Essentials of
Classroom Teaching:
Elementary Language Arts

Essentials of Classroom Teaching
Elementary Language Arts

Margo Wood
University of Southern Maine

SERIES DEVELOPER
C. Alan Riedesel
State University of New York at Buffalo

Allyn and Bacon
Boston   London   Toronto   Sydney   Tokyo   Singapore

Series Editor: Virginia Lanigan
Series Editorial Assistant: Nicole DiPalma
Cover Administrator: Linda Dickinson
Composition Buyer: Linda Cox
Manufacturing Buyer: Louise Richardson
Editorial-Production Service: Colophon Production Service
Cover Designer: Suzanne Harbison
Text Designer: LeGwin Associates

Copyright © 1994 by Allyn and Bacon
A division of Paramount Publishing
160 Gould Street
Needham, Heights, Massachusetts 02194

Library of Congress Cataloging-in-Publication Data
Wood, Margo
    Essentials of classroom teaching: elementary language arts/Margo Wood.
      p.   cm.
    Includes bibliographical references (p.) and index.
    ISBN 0-205-15512-X
    1. Language arts (Elementary)   I. Title. II. Series.
LB 1576.W66   1993   93-33429
372.6'044—dc20   CIP

Printed in the United States of America
10 9 8 7 6 5 4 3 2 1   99 98 97 96 95 94

McLaughe

Contents

Prologue

THE ELEMENTARY SCHOOL POPULATION

The nature of the elementary school population in the United States has changed considerably since today's adults were school children. In general, the student bodies of elementary schools are becoming increasingly diverse; this is a trend that is projected to continue into the twenty-first century. It is likely that the proportion of children from single-parent households will also continue to increase. The percentage of children belonging to ethnic minorities has grown and will continue to grow. William Teale (1989) describes today's elementary school population as "a rich, vibrant mosaic—a dynamic composite of children from a variety of cultures, linguistic backgrounds, and religions "(p.6).

The past 25 years have seen changes in society, family structures, and technology, all of which have profoundly affected children, changing the very nature of childhood and influencing the ways children learn and come to know.

Society

The increased mobility of American families has led to shifting school populations as families move in and out of neighborhoods. The redistributions of people have resulted, in many areas, in a greater mix of races, languages, and cultural backgrounds within classrooms. A positive effect of this is that the perspectives of children have been broadened; they have the opportunity to develop awareness and acceptance of diversity based on first-hand experience. However, diversity can also engender friction, and uprooted children may feel isolated and different.

Family Structure and Lifestyle

An increasing number of families in this country live in such poverty that they find it difficult to provide their children with adequate food, clothing, shelter, and health care. More children than ever before come to school hungry, tired, and stressed. The children who are designated "most disadvantaged" have everyday encounters with homelessness, violent crime, AIDS, and drugs. The so-called advantaged children often live in families that lack enough adults to meet children's emotional needs, or in which adults find too little time for interaction with their children. As a consequence of all this, many of today's children come to school with heavy emotional burdens which sap their energy and interfere with academic learning.

Technology

Today's children are affected by an unprecedented immersion in media and technology. Nearly all children in this country have access to television and radio, and those from more affluent families live in an environment that includes cable TV, computers, and video games. Unrestricted viewing and listening often absorbs large amounts of young children's time, replacing such activities as creative play and reading for pleasure. Children may be quite sophisticated in their ability to use modern technology, but through this technology they are exposed to far more of the adult world than were previous generations of children. In his book *The Disappearance of Childhood*, Neil Postman (1982) describes the loss of innocence that results from the unrestricted flow of media through the lives of young children. They are not protected from the harsher realities of the world until they are old enough to assimilate and understand this information. Graphic depictions of war and violence are standard fare. Images (including distorted and unhealthy ones) of adult sexuality are readily available—sometimes unavoidable.

Educators who are concerned with the effects of this loss of childhood as a protected time are also concerned about the loss of childhood as a time for creative exploration. The entertainment function of television and Nintendo mesmerizes many youngsters. They pass much of their time in passive absorption rather than active exploration of the world around them. James Howe, a children's author, has written, "My greatest worry for children today is that they are losing their capacity to play, to create a city out of blocks, to find a world in a backyard, to dream an adventure on a rainy afternoon. My greatest fear for children today is that they are losing their capacity to play" (1987, p.12).

What are the implications of all this for the teacher of language arts? According to Lucy Calkins, a prominent researcher and writer in the field of literacy, the early childhood and elementary-level language arts curriculum plays a more crucial role than ever before in children's education. Through the reading and sharing of children's literature and through self-exploration and creation in the medium of language, children can regain some of the benefits of play, and teachers can provide effective antidotes to some of the negative influences of the culture that surrounds their students (Calkins, 1991). As their ideas, lives, and stories are valued along with the ideas, lives, and stories of others, they can achieve a measure of the empowerment and validation that are nurturing ingredients in every healthy childhood. The effective teaching of language arts can have an impact on children's lives far beyond that of developing literacy skills, important as those are. Language arts teachers can make a difference.

CONTENT AND STRUCTURE OF THIS TEXT

Following is an overview of the subject matter included in each chapter of this text. From it you will get an idea of what "language arts" actually consists of and previews of the topics treated in each chapter.

Chapter 1: *Language Arts Defined*

This chapter opens with descriptions of two teachers' language arts programs, one at the first-grade and one at the fourth-grade level. These vignettes provide examples of applications of some of the theoretical principles discussed later in the chapter. The components of the language arts program are delineated next. Here you will find a discussion of oral and written communication and of the relationships among language modes. This is followed by a brief history of language arts instruction and presentation of today's goals and curriculum in language arts.

Chapter 2: *How Children Learn Language*

This chapter opens with an explanation of the structure of language, or what it is that children learn when they acquire language. Next we look at the way in which spoken language is learned by children of every race and culture, and the conditions that enable this learning to take place. Literacy acquisition, or the way in which printed language is learned, is similar in many ways to oral language acquisition. The purpose of this part of the chapter is to make you familiar with the developmental sequence of literacy learning and to point out the importance of the conditions for language learning in the context of learning written language.

Chapter 3: *Inside the Classroom*

This chapter addresses characteristics of the classroom that promote effective language arts instruction. The physical layout of the classroom and the arrangement of materials are considered. Two aspects of organization are important: the allotment and structuring of time for instruction and the ways in which students are grouped for instruction. Last, the chapter treats the overall climate of the classroom and how that can affect learning.

Chapter 4: *Oral Communication in the Elementary Classroom*

Two aspects of oral communication are discussed in this chapter. First, we define active listening, which involves attending, assigning meaning, and often generating a response. Particular kinds of participation and response include informational listening, critical listening, and appreciative listening. You will learn the similarities and differences among these kinds of listening.

The second part of the chapter focuses on talk in the classroom. There are special ways to use talk productively in connection with literacy and in content-area learning. Teachers can enhance students' ability to converse and discuss and can help them learn to present interesting, varied oral reports to demonstrate what they have learned and share their knowledge with others.

Chapter 5: *Written Communication: Composing*

This is the first of two chapters on writing. After a discussion of early writing development and how it can be nurtured, the chapter focuses on the writing process and its use in classrooms at various grade levels. The newer way of teaching writing (generally referred to as *the Writing Process approach*) is compared to older methods, in which the teacher's function was largely to assign and correct. You will be introduced to the basic components of the writing process and to ways in which teachers and students work with these within the context of "writing workshop" time in the classroom. Following a section on appropriate expectations for different developmental levels, the discussion focuses on two crucial aspects of the writing workshop: topic selection and writing conferences. The chapter closes with an examination of the teacher's changing roles as instructor, facilitator/manager, and evaluator of writing.

Chapter 6: *Teaching the Conventions of Writing*

This second chapter on writing focuses on helping children acquire the conventions of writing, or correctness of form. Handwriting instruction is discussed first. We look at the forms of writing that may be taught, effective instructional procedures, and tips for working with left-handed writers.

A good deal of the chapter is devoted to spelling; there are many issues and areas of disagreement among educators as to the best way to teach spelling. Our discussion includes spelling development, what is known about effective instruction, and how spelling interfaces with the writing process.

The last section of the chapter is devoted to the issues surrounding grammar instruction. Traditional grammar instruction (analysis of language) is contrasted with instruction in actual usage of correct forms, which receives more emphasis in today's language arts programs.

Chapter 7: *Children's Literature in the Language Arts Curriculum*

Children's literature plays a prominent role in excellent language arts programs. This chapter explores the relationship between children's development and the literature that is most appropriate for them. There are many uses of literature in the curriculum. From literature children gain new insights, learn new information, begin to deal with universal issues, and extend their understanding of other times and cultures. Their responses to literature are examined. The chapter presents the different types or genres of literature that are available, and suggests ways for teachers to keep up with new publications.

Although the chapters in the book vary considerably in length and complexity, they have a consistent structure, which is designed to help you understand and retain the information presented. The first section in each chapter is entitled "Looking Ahead"and gives an overview of the chapter. It is designed to orient you to the subject matter you will read about. Good readers make predictions about reading before launching into new material; the "Looking Ahead" sections will help you to do this. Next in each chapter comes a set of questions entitled "Can You?" These are specific questions about major topics included in the chapter. Most often (especially if you are a novice teacher) you will not know the answers to these questions. This is to be expected. They are not a quiz; rather they are designed to help you set purposes for reading the chapter, since they will be discussed and answered in the body of the chapter. The chapter content ends with a section called "Looking Back," which summarizes the chapter. Following this is a "Self-Test." After studying the chapter, you should be able to generate answers to these questions, many of which require you to synthesize or apply what you have learned. If you have difficulty with a question, refer back to the appropriate section of the chapter and try to find information that will help you. Last of all is the chapter bibliography, in which references cited in the chapter are listed. (*Note: R*eferences for "Prologue" are included in chapter 1 bibliography.)

1 Language Arts Defined

LOOKING AHEAD

Descriptions of the language arts programs of two teachers provide a glimpse of classroom applications of the theoretical content of this text, as well as a reference point for discussions of theory later in the chapter. You will learn about the four language modes—listening, speaking, reading, and writing—and discover how they are integrated in language arts instruction. An historical perspective on language arts teaching is presented, including discussion of the three different models, or belief systems, on which curriculum may be based. The remainder of the chapter is devoted to an examination of the goals of instruction and characteristics of curriculum in language arts that evolved from a coalition of experts in the field who published recommendations for language arts instruction of the future.

CAN YOU?

1. Describe the similarities and differences among the four language modes?

2. Explain three models, or belief systems, that may underlie and shape language arts curricula?

3. Delineate the trends in language arts instruction since 1965?

4. Define the basic goals of language arts instruction?

5. Specify principles that should guide the development of language arts curriculum?

LOOKING IN ON ELEMENTARY CLASSROOMS: PRIMARY

The setup of Louis Benoit's first-grade classroom invites children to explore and learn and to engage in many varied language activities. There is a science center containing a terrarium that is home to two salamanders, collections of interesting rocks and shells, magnifying glasses, magnets and a box of small metal objects, and a pet hamster in a cage, among other things. There are two computer stations and, nearby, a shelf filled with a variety of writing materials and utensils. There is a cozy "reading corner" where the classroom library is housed along with carpet squares, pillows, and two beanbag chairs. Books are not only found in the library corner, however. They are everywhere. Books by a currently featured author line the chalk tray. Beside Louis' desk there is a small replica of a baby's basket, labeled "New Arrivals," that contains the most recently acquired books. There are books about pets beside the hamster's cage and books about shells and magnets in the science center. Near the library corner there is a book spinner containing first-grade favorites, and along one wall are plastic milk cartons containing collections of books that have been sorted by topic or difficulty level and books with home-made covers that have been written by members of the class and published by Louis. In this classroom, books are unavoidable. The walls are covered with children's artwork and writing. A long table is reserved for displaying children's projects.

The school that houses Louis Benoit's first-grade is located in a small New England city. The twenty-one children in his classroom are diverse. The span in age between the oldest and youngest child in the class is nearly two years. Nine of the children live in single-parent households. Five are supported by welfare. Two are from Vietnamese families; no English is spoken in their homes. One is a recent arrival from Ecuador. One child was hospitalized early in the year because of a parental beating; another lives with an abusive, alcoholic mother. Only eight of the twenty-one live in "traditional" families with both biological parents; one of these children will leave this category before the end of the school year. Six of the children began kindergarten in other communities. The class is multiracial and multiethnic. Fifteen years ago such diversity in a class of children was unusual. Today it is the norm.

Every day Louis reads to and with his students and engages them in lively discussions of literature, information, events, and their own experiences. They write every day, recording experiences and feelings in journals in whatever form their literacy development permits. They publish and celebrate their favorite pieces of writing and listen and respond to literature. Each day includes blocks of time devoted to reading and writing as well as literature time.

Several of the children are still in the emergent literacy stage and do not yet read and write conventionally. Others are reading predictable books accurately and writing fluently in a mix of phonetic ("invented") and standard spelling. Louis structures language arts activities in such a way that each child is successful and feels competent and valued as a member of the first-grade community of communicators.

Louis begins the day by reading to his first-graders. He introduces a new picture book every morning and reads it aloud to the children, who are gathered around him on the rug. Next he engages the children in shared reading, using enlarged texts propped up on the easel. As he reads, he follows the print with a small pointer to help the children match speech to print. The children chime in and "read" with him. He reads several predictable "big books" and a poem or chant. Many of these are old favorites that the children know by heart. When he introduces a new reading, he pauses often, giving children the opportunity to predict what is coming next and confirm their predictions. He encourages discussion of the story, characters, and illustrations, and draws the children's attention to features of the print.

At the end of shared reading time, the children choose follow-up activities. Some reread smaller versions of the big books together or with a taped reading at the listening center. Others illustrate parts of a favorite story and write captions for their drawings. Others create story boards out of oaktag, construction paper, and crayons, and retell one of the stories, using stick puppets of the characters which Louis has put out at the retelling center. While the children rotate from one activity to another, Louis works with small groups of children, creating innovative versions of familiar rhymes or simple stories or recording children's dictated stories and using these texts to match words, name letters, and draw conclusions about letter-sound relationships.

If you were to step into Louis' room after a long absence from primary-grade classrooms, you would undoubtedly be struck by his acceptance of children's approximations of reading and writing, the facilitative nature of his role (as opposed to the commander dispensing tasks and information you may remember from your own early school days), and the extent to which children are learning to read and write through activities that have real communicative purposes. The tedious drills and meaningless exercises are gone. In their place is lots of meaningful talking, reading, and writing.

LOOKING IN ON ELEMENTARY CLASSROOMS: INTERMEDIATE

Karen Johnson teaches fourth grade in a rural mid-western community. Her twenty-four students come primarily from working-class families and represent several ethnic backgrounds. Ms. Johnson bases her language arts curriculum on the "authoring cycle" of Jerome Harste and others (Harste and Short, 1988). As she moved toward more literature-based reading instruction and a process approach to teaching writing, she found in the description of the authoring cycle the structure she was looking for. Karen uses the term *authoring* to mean more than writing; she sees it as the process of constructing meaning that can be shared by others. We author when we write, but also when we read and construct our own personal understanding of the writer's words. In addition we author and share meaning through discussion, art, music, and drama.

Karen's students start their day with journal writing, followed by a whole-group planning meeting. The rest of the morning is devoted to authoring through reading and writing. In the afternoon the focus is on math, science, and social studies, all of which include language arts elements as means of constructing and sharing understandings. Karen ends the day with reading aloud from a chapter book and briefly reviewing the day with the children.

The fourth-graders' journals are rather like diaries. The children write personal entries about their lives—their experiences, feelings, or plans. Journal entries often serve as seeds of ideas to be further developed during writing workshop time.

After ten or fifteen minutes for journal writing, Karen calls the class to the large rug at the rear of the classroom where the children sit in a circle. Many bring their journals with them. Those who wish to share read their entries to the group. This sharing is entirely optional, however. The remainder of the group time (about 20 minutes altogether) is spent planning. Karen checks briefly with each group of readers to see how they plan to use their reading time, and informs groups that she plans to work with.

Reading Worktime

Karen gives her students many opportunities to choose what they wish to read and encourages them to respond personally to their reading, but she also believes that at this level children need to explore some literature in depth with other readers. To accomplish this, she has the students work in literature groups and circles. Every few weeks she selects four or five books of the same genre and gives her class a brief booktalk on each, telling a little about the plot and characters. The students choose which of the books they wish to read with a group (there are multiple copies available), and the literature groups are formed. At the group meeting, the children in each group decide how far they will be responsible for reading before they hold a discussion. They do much of this reading during the ensuing sustained silent reading time. When the agreed-upon reading is done, they meet in their literature circles, decide what aspect of the book or chapter they want to discuss, and hold a discussion. At the beginning of the year, Karen modeled appropriate kinds of questions, responses, and group behaviors that facilitate maximum participation, interest, and learning. Sometimes she suggests questions or topics for a group to discuss, but often the children generate discussion topics themselves. Karen has found that fourth-graders for the most part live up to the responsibilities that are given them; by October they have become quite independent and their discussions are usually lively and productive.

Karen goes from group to group, monitoring their progress. She carries a notebook with her and jots brief notes about what each group is doing well or struggling with. On the basis of this information she decides what type of teacher-directed strategy lesson, explanation, or group-process intervention is necessary. When a group is

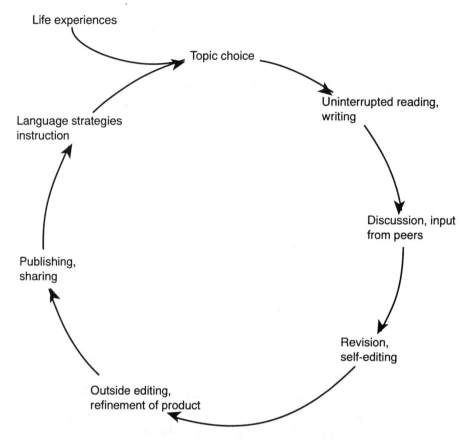

Figure 1-1 The Authoring Cycle.
Adapted from Harste and Short (1988), p.19.

stuck she often helps them make a web of possible topics to discuss, including characters, favorite parts, theme or message, connections between the book and others the children have read, and connections between the book and their own lives.

When each group finishes their book, they plan an extension activity to present to the rest of the class. Popular choices include dramatizations of a part of the story, sequential illustrations, and three dimensional scenes ("shadow boxes"). Because Karen usually plans for a week or two of individualized self-selected reading between these culminating activities and the beginning of the next unit of literature study, the fact that the groups need different amounts of time to finish their reading and activities is not a problem.

Writing Worktime

The hour and a quarter between recess and lunch is devoted to writing instruction in Karen Johnson's classroom. Karen generally begins this period with a brief (5- to 10-minute) minilesson on some aspect of the writing process. (Minilessons and other parts of the writing process are explained in detail in chapters 5 and 6.) She then takes a few minutes to do a status-of-the-class check. As she calls students' names, they tell what piece of writing they will be working on and what stage of the writing process they are in (whether they need to confer with another student or with the teacher or have help with editing, for example). Karen records this information in abbreviated form on a chart. She is thus able to keep track of what all students are doing and how much progress they are making from day to day.

The students then have a sustained silent writing period of about twenty minutes. Everyone is either thinking, planning, drafting ideas onto paper, or rereading and revising. Most of the time the children are writing in a variety of genres on topics of their own choosing. Occasionally Karen suggests or assigns a topic so that her students can share a common experience. Karen is also writing during part of this time, modeling the authoring process and producing writing she can later share with her students as a member of their community of writers. During the last eight or ten minutes of the silent writing time she moves from one student to another, asking quietly, "How's it going?", and giving brief encouragement or facilitating problem solving.

When the twenty minutes are up, some children continue to draft, immersed in their writing. Others find a conference partner and move to one of the four conference stations at the edges of the room to read their drafts to each other. Karen sits at the round table at the front of the room and meets with individuals or groups of children who have completed pieces and are ready for final revisions, editing, or publishing.

The last ten minutes of the writing workshop are reserved for a whole-group share. Once again the children form a circle on the rug to listen to two or three of their classmates share a finished piece or part of a piece and applaud the writer's efforts or give suggestions, if these are solicited by the author.

The structure of Writing Time is flexible. If there is a backlog of children who want to share with the whole class or who need editing conferences or help with publishing, for example, Karen spends extra time as needed and shortens or deletes other parts of the workshop.

COMPONENTS OF THE LANGUAGE ARTS PROGRAM

Traditionally educators have described the goal of language arts instruction as developing students' proficiency in four modes of language: listening, speaking, reading, and writing. These four modes can be compared and contrasted in several ways. It should be noted that for the deaf population visual/spatial language modes are used in place of oral language modes. Watching and signing take the place of listening and speaking. Throughout this discussion of language modes, the comments about listening and speaking hold true for their equivalent processes, watching and signing.

Listening and speaking are oral language modes; reading and writing use written language. The oral language forms are often referred to as *primary* because they are learned informally before children come to school. Although we now know that children in literate environments come to school knowing a good deal about reading and writing, these written language modes are typically considered the school's responsibility and are usually taught more formally. Another way to group the language modes is according to the processing involved. Listening and reading are receptive; they involve constructing meaning from language that comes from another person. Speaking and writing are the expressive modes. They involve constructing a message and conveying it through language. The relationships among the four language modes are illustrated in Figure 1-2.

In order to promote a thorough understanding of the different aspects of language arts, this text contains separate chapters on oral and written language modes. In terms of the way children learn and use language, however, these are artificial divisions. Children do not use different mental processes for listening, speaking, reading, and writing (Smith, 1979). All involve communication, and all involve the construction of meaning. The development of competence in all four modes may be termed *language acquisition*. In good language arts teaching we see several modes used in each activity or in closely related activities. For example, during "read aloud" time, Mr. Benoit's first-graders listen to the story, make predictions and dis-

	RECEPTIVE	PRODUCTIVE
PRIMARY/ ORAL	Listening	Speaking
SECONDARY/ WRITTEN	Reading	Writing

Figure 1-2 The Four Language Modes

cuss the story, and sometimes draw and write about the story. Within their literature groups, Ms. Johnson's fourth-graders plan (speaking, listening, and sometimes writing), read, and discuss (speaking and listening).

In 1976, researcher Walter Loban reported on a longitudinal (13-year) study of the language growth of 338 students from kindergarten through grade 12. One purpose of his study was to examine the differences between students who used language effectively and those who did not. He found positive correlations among the four language modes both in terms of how they developed and how well students used them. Students who were more facile with oral language tended also to develop more competence with written language. Moreover, there was a strong relationship between students' oral language ability and their overall academic achievement. This seminal study demonstrated the clear relationships among the four language modes and the need to address them all in an integrated way in school.

Not only are the four language modes used in an integrated way in language arts instruction; it is also important to realize that the learning and use of language permeates the curriculum and is an integral part of learning in every content area.

AN HISTORICAL PERSPECTIVE ON LANGUAGE ARTS INSTRUCTION

During the early part of the twentieth century, language arts instruction came to be dominated by textbooks or assigned texts, by tests or exams, and to some extent by higher institutions (Dixon, 1991). While listening and speaking were taught tangentially, if at all, reading and writing instruction became dominated by basal readers and language arts texts which emphasized the analysis of language. The assumption was generally made that if students practiced analyzing language and identifying "correct " forms, their use of oral and written language would improve. Stories to be read and compositions to be written were selected and assigned by the teacher. Other characteristics of "old paradigm" language arts instruction included the teaching of spelling (as a distinct subject, divorced from writing) through the memorization of assigned lists of words, which were practiced and tested. Writing was assigned and corrected, but seldom really taught, except for mechanics such as penmanship and punctuation.

To understand the changes that have taken place in language arts instruction over the past fifteen years, it is helpful to be aware of the basic curriculum models upon which language arts instruction may be based. Language arts curricula are conceived, designed, and implemented according to one of three models: the competencies model, the heritage model, and the process or student-centered model (Mandel, 1980; Farrell, 1991). The competencies model reflects the belief that the purpose of language arts instruction is to foster mastery of language skills by the learner. These skills are discrete and are generally perceived to be hierarchical; they must be mastered sequentially. The materials (such as basal readers and graded language arts textbooks) and instructional activities reflect this orientation (Goodman, et al., 1988).

Proponents of the heritage model see the purpose of language arts instruction to be the transmission of the values and traditions of the culture through study of a specified body of literature and guided experiences with various genres and modes of writing. Many of us experienced elementary-level instruction that was based in the competencies model, followed by secondary school programs that exemplified the heritage model. Both of these models tend to be driven by texts and tests. Neither adequately takes into account the fact that the content and skills associated with language arts are not stable. The body of literature continually grows. Scholarship adds to or alters our knowledge of how students attain literacy. Moreover, a great variety of interests, aptitudes, and experiences are represented in the teachers and students who are "doing" the curriculum. It is dynamic and "resists verbal encapsulation" (Farrell,1991, p.63).

The process model differs from the other two in that the curriculum is not determined by tests or texts. Rather, this model has as its purpose the encouragement of language processes that lead to the individual growth of each student in the areas of both competencies and content. Curriculum based on this model is very flexible, since there is no specification of texts or assessment measures that must be used. Reading materials, writing activities, and other language experiences are chosen according to the interests and needs of the students and teacher, and assessment is usually continuous and closely tied to "real" classroom experiences rather than artificial tests (which exist only for the purpose of testing).

According to Mandel (1980), most teachers align their beliefs and practices with one model over the others, and most schools and school districts favor one over the others. Of course all teachers of language arts remain concerned that their students develop competencies in using oral and written language, deepen their understanding of their own culture (and other cultures as well), and engage frequently and productively in the listening, speaking, reading, and writing processes. The three models are not mutually exclusive; however, they represent very different emphases and priorities in language arts instruction. You will find that this text is written from the perspective of one who supports the process model. Development of children's skills in using language will be addressed throughout; however, it will be suggested that skill development is not rigidly hierarchical in nature and that it occurs most appropriately in the context of real, purposeful language activities rather than through exercises and isolated drills. Similarly, the content of language arts that leads to transmission of cultural heritage will be emphasized, particularly in chapter 7, *Children's Literature*. A wide variety of books and activities will be recommended, however, and students' interests will be seen as central to curriculum planning and implementation. The process model of language arts curriculum is, in this author's opinion, the most closely aligned with current understandings about language and literacy development in children. The shift among many theorists and educators toward the process model is seen in the conclusions of the English Coalition Conference of 1987 which came out strongly in favor of the learner-centered curriculum as the appropriate direction for language arts instruction to take in the future.

GOALS OF LANGUAGE ARTS INSTRUCTION

A recent invitational conference sponsored by the National Council of Teachers of English and the Modern Language Association brought educational leaders (including teachers from all levels) together to assess the state of language arts teaching and to suggest directions our teaching of language arts should take in the nineties and beyond. The elementary-level teachers and researchers were charged with producing an agreed-upon set of goals to guide elementary language arts instruction. Their product took the form of a portrait of the student that ideally would emerge from an excellent elementary school language arts program.

The conferees decided against fragmenting their goals into traditional categories (listening, speaking, reading, and writing). Instead they emphasized that students should leave elementary school *knowing about* language, *knowing how* to use language, and *knowing why* language and literacy are crucial to the living of a full and satisfying life. Following is a summary of the part of the conference report that specifies target knowledge, abilities, and attitudes. Upon completion of elementary school, students will

- *Be readers and writers*, experiencing satisfaction and purposeful engagement in these activities. Reading and writing will be an integral part of their everyday lives and will be voluntarily undertaken for their intrinsic value.

- *Use language to understand themselves, others, and their world.* They will use language activities such as listening to or reading stories, writing poetry, or keeping journals as ways of reflecting on their lives and learning about the lives of others.

- *Use language as a tool to get things done.* Their use of oral and written language will help them organize and conduct their lives as productive citizens. They will take in information, form and express opinions, speak and write persuasively.

- *Be competent language users who can speak, listen, read, and write effectively.* In addition to being able to comprehend the literal messages in texts, they will read and listen critically and interpretively. They will have at their command strategies for dealing with unfamiliar words and concepts in the texts they encounter and will be able to respond personally to texts. They will be able both to read and to create a wide variety of types of texts, including essays, narratives, poems, and expository pieces, for different purposes and audiences. They will appreciate literature.

- *Recognize language that is intended to manipulate or control them* and use language effectively in responding to or counteracting such attempts.

- *Become "language theorists,"* knowledgeable about language processes. They will understand and use techniques for creating the effects they want in writing, and they will monitor their purposes and processes when reading. They will be able to self-evaluate their language activities and will have a sense of ownership of language and of membership in a language community.

- *Appreciate and respect others' language and culture.* They will be willing and able to communicate with people whose dialect, language heritage, or culture differs from their own. Having been exposed to a rich variety of literature, experience, and fellow language users, they will be aware of the perspectives of others, and will have an appreciation for both the differences and the commonalties of cultural groups (Teale, 1989).

The recommendations of the consortium conferees for appropriate curriculum grew from these ideas about what student outcomes ideally should be.

THE LANGUAGE ARTS CURRICULUM

Although most educators believe that curriculum should be created at the local level, there are certain principles that are widely recommended as guidelines for developing language arts curriculum.

- *Curriculum should evolve from a sound research knowledge base.* Basic research on child development, learning theory, and language and literacy acquisition should inform the curriculum. The research and writings of Piaget (1926, 1983), Vygotsky (1978,

1986), and Bruner (1977, 1986) are particularly foundational to current thinking about language arts instruction. Building on this is a new body of classroom-based ethnographic research (often referred to as action research) that examines data gathered through careful observation and documentation of what children do in real learning contexts. Researchers of this genre whose work has greatly influenced our understanding of the ways children develop as language users include Heath (1983), Taylor (1983, 1988), Graves (1983), Harste, Woodward and Burke (1984), Calkins (1986, 1991), Atwell, (1987) Cambourne (1987), and numerous classroom teacher-researchers.

Both Louis Benoit's and Karen Johnson's language arts instruction is guided by their knowledge of current theory and research. When they allow students to select their own writing topics, confer with peers about their writing, and publish their best works to be shared, they are acknowledging the work of Graves, Calkins, and Atwell (see chapter 5). Mr. Benoit's acceptance of the less-than-perfect attempts of his first-graders to read and write conventionally reflects his familiarity with the work of Cambourne and others (see chapter 2).

- *The language arts curriculum should be learner-centered.* In other words, the developmental levels, interests, and experiences of students should determine much of the form and content of instruction. Learners need to engage actively in speaking, listening, reading, and writing activities that are meaningful, purposeful, and relevant to their lives. Although commercial publishers can provide useful materials and serve as resources for activities, the most effective language arts programs are not text driven; they are created for and by specific communities of teachers and students.

  Examples of this principle may be seen in Mr. Benoit's classroom. His choices of books to read to his students are based on his knowledge of their development and their interests. He does not read the same books in the same order every year. His students choose what to write about in their journals, and the form of their writing is accepted.

- *The curriculum should emphasize both language products and language processes and treat them as interdependent.* Students learn and practice strategies for improving or extending their ability to discuss, read, or write in the context of actually discussing, reading, and writing for real communicative purposes. Teachers identify strategies and skills to be taught by observing students' language products and determining real needs. A balance is achieved between language use and language analysis.

Karen Johnson, for example, determines topics for whole-class writing mini lessons by observing her students' work. If many children are including dialogue in their stories, she will conduct several mini lessons on the correct use of quotation marks and other conventions of recording conversation. This will help children improve the correctness of their writing products. She will also conduct mini lessons on the effective use of dialogue interspersed with narrative. She will find literature the children are familiar with and point out to them how published authors effectively use dialogue. This adds to their knowledge of the craft of writing and of the process authors use.

- *Language arts instruction should be integrated with other subject areas in the elementary curriculum.* Listening, speaking, reading, and writing can be utilized in connection with every subject area. Integration is a key characteristic of the ideal elementary curriculum, according to many of today's educators. Many teachers organize instruction around themes. For example, second-graders in Ms. Johnson's school who were engaged in a unit on whales read stories and informational books and articles on whales, determined the lengths of various species of whales and measured and marked them out on the playground, listened to recorded whale sounds, tried to capture the essence of "whaleness" through creative movement, created charts and painted murals about whales, reconstructed a mock whale skeleton brought in by a local environmental education organization, wrote letters to legislators to support restrictions on commercial whaling, and wrote stories and informational pieces about whales. The unit led to further study of sea creatures and of endangered species. When the curriculum is organized in this way, content knowledge is developed across the traditional disciplines, while the skills of reading, writing, listening, and speaking are practiced and used for real purposes.

- *An effective assessment program should be an integral part of the language arts curriculum.* The goal of assessment should be the enhancement of students' learning (Johnston, 1987). Therefore, assessment must be in sync with our teaching goals; testing and teaching must be closely related. Structured observations of learners and organized samples of their work must be legitimized as valid and useful forms of evaluation. The recent emphasis on portfolio building as a form of meaningful assessment is an example of the trend toward use of informal assessment of progress over time, based on authentic classroom activities. All the first-grade teachers in Mr. Benoit's district, for example, keep an accordion-style folder for each child. In it is an audio tape on which they record the student reading aloud in November, March, and June. Also included in the folder are periodic samples of the child's writing and a summary of anecdotal notes made while observing the child or reflecting upon his or her growth as a reader and writer.

  According to Teale (1989), "An effective language arts program cannot be based on textbooks or tests. It must be centered on learners and formulated according to sound principles of child learning and sound theories of language and literacy acquisition" (p.15).

LOOKING BACK

A glimpse of language arts instruction in two elementary classrooms was followed by a discussion of the basic premises on which language arts programs are based. There are receptive (listening and reading) and productive (speaking and writing) language modes. All four modes are components of language arts programs and are often integrated by effective teachers. Language arts curricula are increasingly student-centered with attention to language processes developed through real, purposeful language activities rather than through exercises. The goals of language arts instruction are broad and include learning about language and learning how to use language effectively in all four modes. Curriculum arises from these goals, and should be integrated with other subject areas in elementary classrooms.

SELF-TEST

1. Give an example of an activity or series of related activities that would involve students in using three or four language modes.

2. What are the three models or belief systems that may form the basis for language arts curriculum? Which of them characterizes the language arts instruction you experienced as an elementary school student? As a high school student?

3. Suppose you were asked in a job interview to explain your basic goals for language arts instruction. What would you say?

4. Name and explain at least three principles that would guide your development of a language arts curriculum.

BIBLIOGRAPHY

Atwell, N. (1987). *In the middle*. Portsmouth, NH: Heinemann.

Bruner, J.S. (1977). *The process of education*. 2d ed. Cambridge, MA: Harvard University Press.

_____ (1986). *Actual minds, possible worlds*. Cambridge, MA: Harvard University Press.

Calkins, L. (1986). *The art of teaching writing*. Portsmouth, NH: Heinemann.

_____ (1991). *Living between the lines*. Portsmouth, NH: Heinemann.

Cambourne, B. (1987). Language, learning, and literacy. In A. Butler and J. Turbill, *Towards a reading/writing classroom*. Portsmouth, NH: Heinemann.

Dixon, J. (1991). Historical considerations: an international perspective.

Farrell, E.J. (1991). Instructional models for English language arts. In Flood, J., Jensen, J., Lapp, D., and Squire, J. eds. *Handbook of research on teaching the English language arts*. New York: Macmillan.

Goodman, K., Shannon, P., Freeman, Y. and Murphy, S. (1988). *Report card on basal readers*. Katonah, N.Y.: Richard C. Owen Publishers, Inc.

Graves, D. (1983). *Writing: Teachers and children at work*. Portsmouth, N.H.: Heinemann.

Harste, J. and Short, K. (1988). *Creating classrooms for authors: The reading/writing connection*. Portsmouth, N.H.: Heinemann.

Harste, J., Woodward, V. and Burke, C. (1984) *Language stories and literacy lessons*. Portsmouth, N.H.: Heinemann.

Heath, S.B. (1983). *Ways with words*. New York: Cambridge University Press.

Howe, J. (1987). Reflections. *The writing project quarterly newsletter*. 1:3.

Johnston, P. (1987). Assessing the process, and the process of assessment, in the language arts. In J. Squire (ed.).*The dynamics of language learning* (335-357). Urbana, Ill: National Conference on Research in English/ERIC Clearinghouse on Reading and Copmmunication Skills.

Mandel, B.J. (1980). *Three language arts curriculum models*. Urbana, Ill: NCTE

Piaget, J. (1926). *The language and thought of the child*. London: Routledge and Kegan Paul.

_____ (1983). "Piaget's Theory." in *Handbook of child psychology*, ed. P.H. Mussen. *Vol I, History, theory, and methods*, ed. W. Kessen. New York: John Wiley & Sons.

Postman, N. (1982). *The disappearance of childhood*. New York: Delecorte Press.

Smith, F. (1976). The Language arts and the learner's mind. *Language Arts*. 56, 118-125.

Stone, E. (1990). Making learning real for intermediate kids. In Mills, H. and Clyde, J.A., eds. *Portraits of whole language classrooms*. Portsmouth, NH: Heinemann.

Taylor, D. (1983). *Family literacy*. Portsmouth, N.H.: Heinemann.

Taylor, D. and Dorsey-Gaines, C. (1988). *Growing up literate.* Portsmouth, NH: Heinemann.

Teale, W (1989). Language arts for the 21st century. J. Jensen, ed. *Stories to grow on.* Portsmouth, N.H.: Heinemann.

Vygotsky, L.S. (1978). *Mind in society.* Cambridge, Mass.: Harvard University Press.

_____ (1986). *Thought and language.* Cambridge, MA: MIT Press.

2 How Children Learn Language

LOOKING AHEAD

Literacy learning is, in fact, language learning. For this reason we examine first the components of language that are learned by children as they acquire speech, the general pattern of oral language acquisition, and the principles and conditions that are characteristic of language learning. This background is intended to help you understand the discussion of literacy development which follows. Children pass through predictable stages as they become competent users of written language; it is helpful for teachers to be aware of these stages with their varying instructional goals. The last part of the chapter asks you to reexamine the conditions for language learning in the context of literacy acquisition. Knowledge and creation of these conditions in classrooms is essential to effective language arts instruction.

CAN YOU?

1. Define and describe the components of spoken language?

2. Name seven conditions that are crucial to language learning?

3. Describe the stages children pass through as they learn to read and write?

4. Compare oral language learning to literacy acquisition?

5. Explain how to incorporate conditions for literacy learning in an elementary classroom?

THE STRUCTURE OF LANGUAGE: WHAT IS LEARNED

Language enables children to learn about the world, to control it to some extent, to interact with others, and to express their individuality. Learning to talk involves developing implicit knowledge of four aspects of language: the phonological, syntactic, semantic, and pragmatic systems.

The *phonological system* is the sound system of the language. Approximately 40 discrete speech sounds are used in English. These speech sounds are referred to as *phonemes* and are written inside diagonal lines (/p/, /a/). The letter or combination of letters that represents a phoneme is called a *grapheme*. Alternative graphemes may represent the same phoneme. For example, the *ai* in paint, the *a* in gate, and the *ea* in steak are all graphemes that stand for the phoneme /a/.

The phonological system is largely mastered by the time a child comes to school. However a few sounds, notably /v/, /th/, /ch/, and /sh/ in medial and final positions in words, typically are not acquired until after age five or six. It is not uncommon for seven- or eight-year-olds to continue to make some sound substitutions, especially in consonant clusters ("cwank" for "crank," for example) (Tompkins and Hoskisson, 1991).

The *syntactic system* comprises the grammar of the language, the rules that determine how words are combined to form sentences. By the time children enter school, they have acquired the basic grammatical rules of their language and are capable of generating sentences of almost infinite variety. During the elementary school years, their syntactic development continues. They use a greater variety of sentence patterns and make use of complex sentences containing dependent clauses. Whereas a primary-grade student would be likely to use *and* or *then* to connect ideas ("My dog is brown and white and he always chases cats and his name is Silky."), an older student would be likely to embed some of these ideas ("My brown and white dog, Silky, always chases cats.").

The meaning of the language is contained in the *semantic system*, which consists of the language user's vocabulary. As a person acquires new concepts and the words that represent them, the semantic aspect of language develops. Lindfors (1987) warns that "word counts" of known vocabulary can only be rough estimates, since there are degrees of "knowing" a word. Nevertheless, estimates of vocabulary show the rapidity of language growth in the semantic aspect during childhood. Entering kindergartners are estimated to have an average of approximately 5000 words in their vocabularies; they add approximately 3000 words per year through the elementary grades (Tompkins and Hoskisson, 1991).

Pragmatics refers to the social/cultural aspects of language use. How we talk or write is influenced by our purpose and audience, by the function the language is intended to serve. Variations in language, known as *dialects*, occur among geographic regions, ethnic groups, and socioeconomic classes. Children naturally acquire the dialect of the community in which they are raised. The language of power in this country is Standard American English, the form of the language most often used in books, magazines and newspapers, on television, and in schools. The term *nonstandard English* applies to other dialects including the English spoken in urban ghettos, rural New England, and southwestern Hispanic communities, to name just a few. These dialects are nonstandard alternatives to Standard American English that reflect the communities of their speakers; however, they are not substandard or inferior in any linguistic sense, merely different in some aspects of phonology, syntax, and semantics. In order for children to learn to use language effectively and successfully, it is essential that school personnel convey acceptance of each child's dialect. Disapproval of language amounts to disapproval of family, culture, and community, and can be extremely destructive to children's self-concepts.

Children come to school speaking the language of their family and community. At school they are exposed to standard English, which may be quite similar to or quite different from the dialect they have acquired at home. Their pragmatic development includes learning to vary the language they speak or write depending on their purpose and intended audience. M.A.K. Halliday (1973) has delineated seven categories of language function:

1. Instrumental language—language to satisfy needs
   Example: "I want a drink of water."

2. Regulatory language—language to control the behavior of others
   Example: "Put the crayons in the box."

3. Interactional language—language to establish and maintain social relationships
   Example: "Do you want to play with me?"

4. Personal language—language to express personal opinions
   Example: "I like the red shirt better than the blue one."

5. Imaginative language—language to express imagination and creativity
   Example: "The stars look like diamonds."

6. Heuristic language—language to seek information and find out about things
   Example: "What does the snake eat?"

7. Informative language—language to convey information
   Example: "There are five people in my family."

During the elementary grades, children learn to use language for a wide variety of functions. They also learn the written language counterparts of oral language functions. (For example, interactional language would appear in friendly letters or dialogue journals, the written parallels of conversations and oral sharing.) This is accomplished by facilitating children's use of language for genuine communication and for interacting with others.

ACQUISITION OF SPOKEN LANGUAGE

Learning to understand and speak the language of the culture into which one is born is undoubtedly the most impressive single learning feat of one's life. If you, as an adult native English speaker, set out today to learn Japanese, Polish, Swahili, or any of the several thousand languages spoken in the world, you will find the task immensely difficult and complex. Every language is a unique composite of the structural and pragmatic elements described previously, with many idiosyncrasies and nuances. And yet toddlers and preschoolers, whose brains are "immature," learn whichever of these languages surrounds them, with success and relative ease. How do they do this?

Some theorists contend that the ability to use language is innate to humans and unfolds naturally with maturation, provided there is language in the environment (Chomsky, 1965; Lenneberg, 1967). Others view language acquisition as being primarily dependent on cognitive development. They suggest that children have a general capacity for inference and ability to solve problems that enables them to learn language (Slobin, 1979; Donaldson,1979). Vygotsky (1962) noted that social interactions play a crucial role in language acquisition. The "interactionist view" of language learning stresses that children do indeed engage their cognitive abilities to make sense of the world, but that they are distinctly social beings; language is needed and used by them for communicating with others (Genishi and Dyson, 1984; Lindfors, 1987). These theories are not mutually exclusive. The human brain does seem to be "programmed" to learn language at an early age. However, children who are denied the conditions under which language normally is learned fail to learn any language at all. Probably you have heard stories of "feral" children such as the Wild Boy of Averon or of other children who spent their early years in language-deprived environments and did not learn to speak. Although maturation certainly plays a role in language development, the importance of the environment in stimulating and promoting language development is clear. Children acquire their oral language in an environment that is rich with its use. They construct necessary knowledge about language in the context of social interaction.

As they learn and use language, children make many "errors," if their language is compared to that of adult speakers. However, such errors are an integral part of the process of learning how language works. With continued feedback from other language users in the environment, children's language more and more closely approximates adult speech patterns. Oral language development constitutes a basis for literacy. It makes learning to read and write possible.

Current research on language and literacy development is based on close observation of children. We are now aware of many of the strategies that enable children to learn language. One of the most important insights about language learning is that it is an active process that involves problem solving. Children create hypotheses about language and then interact with the people who are generating language all around them. Language learning is not a passive or purely imitative process. Children actually construct and reconstruct language as they learn to use it. We now realize that reading and writing are language processes and therefore are closely tied to oral language and learned in much the same way. For this reason it is important for teachers to be familiar with the principles and patterns of oral language acquisition (Morrow, 1989).

In general, observers of young children note that understanding and use of oral language proceeds from whole to part. Babies' first seeming attempts to use language for communicative purposes typically consist of global imitations based on the way language sounds and the way it is used (the whole). The "babbling" of most eight- to ten-month-olds includes varied intonations (questioning, demanding, stating) and social conventions, such as turn-taking. There are, however, no identifiable words or phrases (the parts). Children appear to acquire first a gestalt for language, a general understanding of its nature and purpose.

An important event in language development (from the parents' perspective, particularly) is the child's production of an identifiable word. In most cases children's early pronunciation of words consists of gross approximations whose meaning is guessed by adults from the context in which the word is uttered and other cues (such as pointing) given by the child. For example, if a toddler urgently repeats, "ba-ba, ba-ba," as he reaches toward his bottle, which is sitting on the table, his mother assumes he is saying "bottle" and is likely to reinforce this by using the word as she responds to what she presumes to be the child's meaning.

"You want your bottle, Jimmy? O.K., here's your bottle. Jimmy's bottle." As she speaks she places the bottle in Jimmy's outstretched hands. Caregivers tend to respond with excitement and encouragement to children's early attempts to produce words, focusing on the meaning of the utterance.

Single-word utterances are followed by combinations of two or three words which are often referred to as *telegraphic speech*. Meaning is condensed into brief phrases whose full meaning must be inferred from context, tone of voice, and accompanying actions. "Allgone milk," for example, may mean, "My cup is empty; I have finished my milk," "My milk spilled," or "I want to get down from the highchair and play now." The phrases used by children in this stage of their development are not imitations of adult speech, nor are they randomly constructed. The child orders words consistently to conform to rules that he or she has created. For example, the child who uses "allgone milk" is likely to say "allgone Mommy," "allgone bath," or "allgone truck," but not "bath all gone."

During the preschool years, children's language growth is extremely rapid. Vocabulary increases dramatically, and the basic syntax or grammar of the language is acquired. It is interesting that most grammatical forms and conventions are mastered in a relatively short time through interaction with others. This feat is not accomplished as the result of conscious teaching by adults, or even by direct imitation; rather, it appears to result from a problem-solving process (Lindfors, 1987). Children detect patterns in language and form implicit hypotheses about language structures from their exposure to the quantities of language in their environment. The language structures they use reflect these hypotheses. As they hear more and more language, they revise their hypotheses until their language structures conform more closely to the models around them. Many children, for example, generalize the formation of past tense by adding *ed* to verbs. They produce verb forms they have not heard used by adults: "We bringed our toys." "I goed with Daddy." With further language experience and exposure to irregular past tense forms used by the speakers in their environment, they qualify their use of the past tense rule. Moreover, this happens not as a result of correction of form (which is likely to have little or no effect on the child's language structures) but through repeated exposure, with attention always on meaning.

The sequence of oral language development can be summarized in extremely simplified form, as follows:

- Random utterances of sounds

- Global imitation of speech sounds and patterns

- Single-word utterances

- Telegraphic speech

- Production of full sentences

- Expanding repertoire of sentence variety, vocabulary, and pragmatic functions

PRINCIPLES AND CONDITIONS OF LANGUAGE LEARNING

Two general principles of language learning become apparent as one observes this sequence of language development: (1) Language learning proceeds from whole to part. (2) Language learning involves problem solving, the formation and testing of hypotheses (O'Donnell and Wood, 1992). These principles describe *cognitive characteristics* of language learning. In addition to this knowledge, we now are fully aware of the *conditions* that lead to effective language learning. In the 1970s Australian researcher Brian Cambourne spent hundreds of hours observing children who were learning to talk and studying their interactions with the adults in their environments. His documentation of observed behaviors resulted in identification of seven conditions for language learning, which have come to be known as Cambourne's Conditions. He named these conditions *immersion, demonstration, expectation, responsibility, use, approximation, response*, and *engagement* (Cambourne, 1987).

According to Cambourne, "In order to learn to talk one must not only be human, but certain conditions must operate to permit that learning to occur" (Cambourne, 1987, p. 6). These conditions appear to apply to all kinds of language learning including learning to read and write and learning a second language; moreover they are transferable to classroom practice. Therefore it is imperative that teachers be thoroughly familiar with them. Let us examine them one by one.

Immersion

From the moment of their birth, children are immersed in language. It is as integral a part of their environment as the arms of the adults who hold them and the food that appears when they are hungry. Language flows around them during most of their waking hours (and many of their sleeping hours as well, in some cultures). They are surrounded by proficient users of the language they will eventually learn. The sounds, rhythms, and meanings of this language are all around them. Moreover, the language they hear is meaningful, purposeful, and whole. The language-users around them do not generally talk nonsense or speak in fragments.

Demonstration

A demonstration is a model. Language-users in a child's environment provide thousands of demonstrations of functional, meaningful uses of the spoken form of the language. Models and examples abound. The toddler sitting in her high chair, for example, hears a stream of sounds issue from her mother's mouth and sees her father, in response, pass the bowl of mashed potatoes. This type of demonstration is observed in many, many situations, but is also repeated in similar contexts over and over, modeling the conventions that are used to express meaning through language. The learner thus is provided with vast amounts of data to use in incorporating these conventions for her own use in comprehending and producing language.

Expectation

Everyone in the child's environment expects him to learn to talk, as surely as they expect him to learn to walk and to feed himself with a spoon. Unless a child is born with severe disabilities, the expectation that he will acquire these behaviors is actually an assumption by parents—of course he will learn to talk. Cambourne maintains that expectations constitute a subtle form of communication which learners "pick up" and which influences their learning. In teaching their children to swim, for example, some parents convey by their anxious tone and demeanor and their insistence on regular drill and practice that learning to swim is hard, is dangerous, and is not accomplished by everyone. Children who attempt to learn to swim under these conditions are often anxious and in fact do find learning to swim very difficult or impossible.

We do not communicate the expectation that learning to talk is difficult or that the child may not be capable of accomplishing it. Therefore even children who learn to talk later than average do not experience the anxiety or pressure that unnecessarily retards or inhibits learning. Their parents convey that they fully expect that spoken language will eventually be mastered, and it is.

Responsibility

Parents and other caregivers to preschoolers do not plan a sequential curriculum in oral language. Children have the full responsibility for the pace and order of their language learning: it is internally (though, of course, not consciously) determined. Can you imagine a parent saying, "Betsy isn't using possessive pronouns yet, so that is the element we will model for her and drill her on for the next few weeks."? We find the very idea humorous and far-fetched. Children master specific grammatical constructions at different ages and in different combinations and sequences. By the age of 5 or 6, however, the great majority have reached the same general state of language knowledge and use. Because their learning is natural, they reach the same destination by different routes. If we were try to take over the responsibility for their acquisition of speech and lead them all along a sequential, logical (to us) path, our children very likely would not learn to talk.

Approximation

Children's earliest utterances of identifiable words generally are gross approximations (such as "baba" for "bottle"), yet adults react to them with delight and encouragement and are proud that their child has begun to talk. No one expects toddlers to speak with the precision and correctness of adults; approximation is expected, accepted, and encouraged. Caregivers attempt to decipher the meaning of the child's speech and respond to that; the form is not commented on. If we analyzed the deficits in their grammatical constructions and corrected their pronunciation, they would undoubtedly talk much less. Our acceptance of approximation in their language is closely tied to our expectation that they will learn to talk. We know that their approximations will come closer and closer to adult speech as they hear and use language over a period of time; therefore it is a non-issue.

Employment

Children who are learning to talk have unlimited opportunities to use the medium of oral language. Imagine what would happen if, daily, they were restricted to one or two twenty- or thirty-minute periods designated as "talk time." Not only would this be unnatural, but it would not provide anywhere near the amount of practice needed to master the conventions of the language. In the real world, children talk throughout the day in conjunction with nearly everything they do. They practice the conventions of spoken language frequently and freely, whenever they wish to communicate.

Feedback

Children move from gross approximations of single words to phrases to complete sentences in the context of a great deal of feedback of a special kind. As caregivers respond to young children, they tend to do two things: they often repeat the child's message in expanded form, modeling the adult use of conventions in a completely nonthreatening way, and they respond to the child's intended meaning. For example:

Toddler: I eated all my pear.

Adult: Yes you did. You ate all your pears. Do you want some more?

Toddler: Dat Annie su.

Adult: Yes, that's your shoe, Annie. Let's find the other one.

Adults who give this sort of feedback expect to do it for a long time. They know that immature forms of speech will continue to be used until the child is ready to change them. One never hears a parent say in an exasperated tone, "The past tense form of 'eat' is 'ate.' How many times do I have to model that for you?" or "I've showed you and showed you how to use possessive forms. Why don't you pay attention and get it right?" Modeling must be repeated over and over again; however, we do not naturally draw attention to the differences between the child's speech and our own. Rather, we put the focus of our feedback where it belongs: on meaning.

As you learn about literacy development, you will see that Cambourne's research into the conditions for language learning is of great relevance to teachers who are attempting to help young children learn to read and write, for literacy learning is a language-learning process. Although the language is in written form, the same conditions apply to its acquisition.

LITERACY ACQUISITION

Literacy learning is a developmental process which begins long before the child enters school. As children progress from generic understandings and rough approximations to proficient use of print, they pass through discernible stages of growth (O'Donnell and Wood, 1992). Awareness of these stages, with their unique learner characteristics and instructional goals, gives teachers a framework that is helpful in designing developmentally appropriate instruction. Note that these developmental designations are not tied to age or grade level; a fourth-grader may be in the initial stage, or a second-grader may have progressed to basic literacy. However, general grade-level equivalents are mentioned in the following stage descriptions to help give a sense of "typical" development.

Emergent Literacy Stage

One of the principles stated earlier in this chapter is that language learning proceeds from whole to part. Children in the emergent stage of literacy development are acquiring various understandings about print: what it is for, how it looks, how it is used by adults, and how it relates to their lives. A general understanding of the nature and purpose of print is an essential prerequisite to learning to match speech to print in the conventional manner.

Most preschoolers and kindergartners are in the emergent stage. Our goals for children in this stage are that they will

- Seek out and enjoy experiences with books and print

- Become familiar with the language of literature and the patterns of stories

- Understand and follow the sequence of stories read to them

- Experiment with reading and writing independently, through approximation

- See themselves as developing readers and writers

- Begin to acquire some specific understandings about print (for example, that printed language consists of letters that are grouped in words separated by spaces).

In order for these goals to be realized, young children must be immersed in a literate environment; they must see reading and writing modeled and enjoyed, they must be read to frequently, they must be invited to retell, dramatize, and illustrate stories, and they must be encouraged to experiment with writing. Some preschoolers are fortunate enough to live in such a literate environment or to receive daycare from adults who realize the value of literacy activities and provide appropriate experiences. While realizing the importance of efforts to educate parents and daycare providers about the vital contribution they can make to their children's future success in school and beyond, teachers' focus is on what is done with and for children who have already begun their formal schooling. We can at least ensure that all children, regardless of their preschool experiences, are immersed in a rich and appropriate literacy environment during their early school years. More detailed discussions and suggestions for implementing such programs will be found in later chapters of this book.

Initial Reading and Writing Stage

Most children pass through the initial stage during their first- and second-grade years. They begin to match speech and print more conventionally. We know they have entered the initial stage when they begin to identify words or phrases that are very familiar or highly meaningful to them. Typically these are names (their own and family members'), labels (Pepsi, STOP, Cheerios), and other high-meaning words (love, cat). As they are repeatedly exposed to familiar printed texts, children in this stage increase the number of words they can identify easily and learn to use strategies to figure out the words they do not recognize at sight. They typically make extensive use of syntactic cues, or language patterns, and semantic (meaning) cues in the surrounding text, and gradually learn to use their knowledge of graphophonics (letter-sound correspondences) as well to construct meaning from the text.

Ideally, predictable, familiar texts are used for initial reading instruction and practice. Appealing stories with real, interesting story lines and predictable language, simple rhymes, songs, poems, and chants, and the children's own transcribed language are all appropriate materials for helping initial readers increase their sight vocabularies (words immediately recognized) and practice the use of effective word-identification strategies. Teachers often use enlarged versions of these texts, either teacher-made or commercially produced, that can be seen easily by everyone in a group as the teacher reads along with the children, following the text with a pointer.

Initial-stage learners are encouraged to write independently, spelling as best they can using their knowledge of letter-sound correspondences. Drawing is typically a major part of the composition process for writers at this stage. Responses to their writing focus on the meaning, and correctness of spelling and form are required only if the writing is to be "published," or shared with a larger audience (in which case the teacher or another adult does most of the editing for the student).

The major goals for students in the initial stage are

- To view reading and writing as meaning-making processes

- To develop "sight" vocabulary

- To use context and graphophonic cues in reading and writing

- To see themselves as readers and writers

Transitional Stage

The transitional stage of literacy development marks a unique period between beginning attempts to read and write and fluent independent reading and writing. Children who are entering this stage have acquired considerable sight vocabulary and are able to use word-identification strategies as they read. Although they can figure out many words independently (in context), their reading tends to be slow and laborious because they have to pause frequently to puzzle-out words that are still unfamiliar in printed form. Their written compositions are longer than those produced in the initial stage, and spelling is most often a mix of phonetic "invented" spelling and standard spelling. With experience and practice, students at this stage are capable of making rapid progress in reading and writing.

The major goals for students in this stage are

- To increase fluency in reading and writing

- To continue to focus on meaning in reading and writing

- To maintain motivation to read and write

These goals are best accomplished in settings where children have daily opportunities to spend extended periods of time reading materials that are of interest to them and that are fairly easy for them to read independently. They also need daily opportunities to write, both as a form of self-expression and in connection with their reading and with other content-area study. Above all else, transitional-stage students need practice and application. They literally learn to read and write by reading and writing. They need to share both their reading and their writing and to feel that their compositions and responses are valued. Most children pass through the transitional stage between second and fourth grades.

Some children develop fluency in reading more quickly than in writing. For a few children, the opposite is true. By the time they leave the transitional stage, however, the vast majority have achieved considerable fluency in both modes.

Basic Literacy Stage

Students entering the basic literacy stage have acquired enough fluency to be able to concentrate fully on the content of their reading and writing, with minimal attention to the acts of reading and writing. The majority of fourth- to sixth-graders are in this stage. They are able to read an increasing variety of materials independently, write in various genres, and use their reading and writing competencies for different purposes. In their narrative and informational reading, students now encounter word meanings and concepts that are outside of their experiences. They become capable of extensive revision of their writings, and take on more and more responsibility for editing for correct form.

Major goals for students at the basic literacy stage are

- To expand breadth of experience in reading and writing

- To comprehend increasingly complex reading materials

- To extend meaning vocabulary

- To develop awareness and use of strategies for reading, writing, and studying

The literacy curriculum at this stage includes both teacher-directed and student-selected reading and writing, direct instruction and guided practice in reading and writing strategies and vocabulary development, and ample opportunities to use both reading and writing in connection with content-area learning.

An important result of successful passage through this stage is the establishment of permanent literacy. Even if schooling is discontinued and reading and writing are not extensively practiced, basic reading and writing competencies will not deteriorate appreciably (Powell, 1977). For this reason, the attainment of a sixth-grade equivalency level in reading is one accepted benchmark of minimal, or "functional," literacy. In other words, if a person is able to read materials that could be read and understood by an average sixth-grader, he or she is capable of performing most of the reading and writing tasks required for everyday living (reading and responding to want ads, reading notes sent home by teachers, using recipes, and following directions for taking medications, for example).

Refinement Stage

Students whose literacy development is rather typical and who have had appropriate language arts instruction through the elementary grades usually enter the final stage of literacy by sixth or seventh grade. They literally refine and extend the competencies acquired in the basic literacy stage. They develop higher-level reading and thinking competencies as they interact with increasingly abstract materials. Their vocabularies continue to expand, and reading rate and flexibility increase. Their writing becomes more polished and sophisticated; they are able to write about topics that are further removed from their own experiences and convey their "movement of mind" to their readers. The refinement stage is extremely important in overall literacy growth; it is during this stage that students become able to deal with specialized subjects and technical information (a prerequisite for higher education and for many jobs) as well as to use reading and writing for personal growth and enjoyment. Students who do reach this stage are likely to continue to refine their reading (and less often, their writing) throughout their lives. Those who do not progress into the refinement stage are unlikely to realize their full potential as readers and writers.

PRINCIPLES AND CONDITIONS OF LITERACY LEARNING

The principles and conditions of language learning that were discussed in connection with oral language acquisition hold true for literacy learning as well. We noted, for example, that *language is learned from whole to part*. In the domain of printed language, this principle may be seen in children's earliest attempts to read and write. The foundation for later learnings is a general understanding of what print looks like and how it is used in the world of literate people. The preschooler who turns the pages of a familiar book, retelling the story in his own words, or the child who writes a string of letter-like marks beside her drawing and "reads" her message to a friend are showing their general understanding of the print medium. Later they will become familiar with and able to use the parts.

The second principle of language learning is that *it is a problem-solving process*. As children gain exposure to the world of printed language, they begin to detect patterns, to "puzzle-out" how print and speech are related, and to discover print conventions. This is particularly evident in their early writings. Young children go through phases when they use letter-names as letter-sounds, for example (NHR for "nature," or LFNT for "elephant"). This behavior disappears from their writing as they gain experience and discover that that particular strategy is not used in standard English spelling.

Cambourne's conditions for oral language learning are crucial to literacy learning as well.

Immersion

Children learn to talk in an environment where they are surrounded by talk that is meaningful, purposeful, and whole. In order to acquire literacy, children need to be immersed in printed language that is meaningful, purposeful, and whole. The massive amounts of data they need to make sense of print are provided by the presence of books, newspapers and magazines, by adults reading books aloud to them regularly and frequently, and by observations of adults reading and writing and using print in the environment (traffic and street signs, ads, labels).

Demonstration

Just as speech is constantly modeled for children who are learning to talk, reading and writing must be demonstrated on a daily basis by literate people in the children's environment. Just as the modeling of speech takes place in the context of real, functional talking, the modeling of reading and writing should be in the context of real literacy activities such as reading for pleasure and information, and writing to order and manage (making a grocery list) or communicate (writing a letter). Children from literate environments—environments in which reading and writing are an integral part of the everyday lives of the adults around them—generally learn to read and write sooner and more easily than those who are not exposed to this type of environment. Regardless of the types of environments children come from, we can make sure that their school classrooms are rich literacy environments and that they encounter frequent modeling and demonstration of every aspect of the reading and writing processes.

Expectation

As teachers, we must believe and convey our belief to children that all of them will learn to read and write, just as surely as they all learned to talk. Too many adults lack conviction on this point and convey anxiety over children's progress with literacy learning, particularly if it is not as rapid as the adult thinks it should be. Although children will master the conventions of written language at very different rates (just as they learn to talk at different rates), all except those who are developmentally disabled or suffer from rare mental or cognitive disorders can eventually become functionally literate, given the necessary conditions for language learning.

Responsibility

Although there are general developmental stages that children pass through as they learn to read and write, there is no predetermined order in which they master the conventions of print. Detailed case studies of many individual children have shown us that they take amazingly individual routes to reach the same destination. Effective teachers facilitate language learning by taking cues from children about what they know and what they seem ready to attempt and by providing opportunities for them to extend their learning through observation and practice. The determination of pace and order of learning is left to the learner.

Approximation

Approximation is a necessary and natural phenomenon of language acquisition. We tend to accept this as a matter of course in speech development, but to mistrust it in the context of literacy acquisition. Too often in the past, children have been expected to display immediate adult competence in using the conventions of reading and writing. Children who learn to read and write naturally begin by imitating (very crudely, at first) the processes. With lots and lots of modeling and experience, they gradually move toward accuracy. If their early attempts are accepted (as are their early attempts at speech), they will proceed with confidence. If, however, their early attempts are consistently evaluated for correctness, children will lose their confidence and hesitate to take risks or try new experiences in reading and writing, for fear of making mistakes.

Employment

American schools have been criticized for allowing students far too little time to engage in sustained reading and writing (Anderson, et. al., 1985). We know that the quantity of reading and writing done by students correlates highly with their achievement in these areas (and indeed in all school subjects). During the stage of their lives when they are learning to talk, children have almost constant opportunities to use oral language. Similarly, they need many, many opportunities to practice the conventions of reading and writing for equally real communicative purposes. Listening to real stories read aloud, reading real books and articles, and writing for real audiences must be daily occurrences for children if they are to develop literacy as fully and as easily as is possible.

Feedback

Teachers can be of most help to beginning readers and writers by responding to meaning, first and foremost, and by repeatedly modeling conventional forms. The teacher who writes a meaningful response to a child's journal entry, using some of the words he spelled unconventionally (thus modeling their standard spellings), is using this kind of feedback. She may have to model the standard spelling of the same words many times before she sees changes in the child's spelling; she accepts this and continues to model within meaningful writing situations.

As you read through Cambourne's conditions for language learning, it may strike you that they seem most applicable at the emergent and initial stages of literacy development. In actual fact, however, they are applicable, with some variations, to more advanced literacy learning as well. While older, more accomplished readers and writers can profit from more analysis of written language, and from specific instruction on use of conventions and strategies, both learning and motivation are most evident in classrooms where the teacher's primary focus is on meaning, and where students' reading and writing products not only are worked on, but also are ultimately shared and celebrated.

LOOKING BACK

Parallels between oral language learning and literacy acquisition have been pointed out in this chapter. The principles and conditions of language learning apply to all language learning, oral and written. Two important principles are the "whole-to-part" principle and the "problem-solving process" principle. Cambourne's conditions of language learning include immersion, demonstration, expectation, responsibility, approximation, employment, and feedback.

As students acquire literacy, they pass through several discernable stages that are fairly invariant, but are not dependent on age or grade level. The stages described are Emergent Literacy, Initial Reading and Writing, the Transitional stage, the Basic Literacy stage, and the Refinement stage. The reading and writing behaviors of students in each stage are different, as are the general instructional goals that are appropriate. Knowledge of these stages helps teachers determine where students are and what they need. By combining this information with a knowledge of the conditions that promote literacy learning, teachers have a sound basis for facilitating each student's growth in language arts.

SELF-TEST

1. Define the phonological, syntactic, semantic, and pragmatic systems of language.

2. Describe three ways in which you think the knowledge of the principles and conditions of language learning described in this chapter will influence your teaching of language arts.

3. Suppose you are a first-grade teacher. A parent comes to see you, concerned that her daughter's writing contains misspellings that you have not corrected. Explain to her the condition of "approximation" and draw parallels with her daughter's oral language development.

4. How might your familiarity with the stages of literacy development affect your expectations of individual children in your class?

5. Look at the reading and writing of an elementary school child you know. What stage would you estimate the child is in? Why?

BIBLIOGRAPHY

Anderson, R. C., Hiebert, E., Scott, J., & Wilkinson, I. (Eds.). (1985). Becoming a *nation of readers*. Washington, D.C.: National Institute of Education.

Cambourne, B. (1987). Language, learning and literacy. In Butler, A. and Turbill, J. *Towards a reading-writing classroom*. Portsmouth, N.H.: Heinemann, 5 - 10.

Chomsky, N. (1965). *Aspects of a theory of syntax*. Cambridge, Mass.: MIT Press.

Donaldson, M. (1979). *Children's minds*. New York: W.W. Norton & Company.

Genishi C. and Dyson, A.H. (1984). *Language assessment in the early years*. Norwood, N.J.: Ablex Publishing Corporation.

Halliday, M.A.K. (1973). *Explorations in the functions of language*. London: Edward Arnold.

Lenneberg, E. (1967). *Biological foundations of language*. New York: John Wiley.

Lindfors, J. (1987). *Children's language and learning*. (2nd ed.) Englewood Cliffs, N.J.: Prentice-Hall.

Morrow, L.M. (1989). *Literacy development in the early years*. Englewood Cliffs, N.J.: Prentice-Hall.

O'Donnell, M. and Wood, M. (1992). *Becoming a reader: a developmental approach to reading instruction*. Boston: Allyn and Bacon.

Powell, W.W. (1977). Levels of literacy. *Journal of Reading*, 20 (6), 488-492.

Slobin, D. (1979). *Psycholinguistics*. (2nd ed.) Glenview Ill.: Scott Foresman and Company.

Tompkins, G. and Hoskisson, K. (1991). *Language arts content and teaching strategies* (2nd ed.). New York: Macmillan.

Vygotsky, L. S. (1962). *Thought and language*. Cambridge, Mass.: MIT Press.

3   Inside the Classroom

LOOKING AHEAD

One of the goals of a classroom teacher is to create an environment in which language arts flourish and children grow as language learners and users. Louis Benoit and Karen Johnson have achieved this goal (see chapter 1). Their classrooms may seem quite idealistic; however, classrooms like theirs do exist. In this chapter classrooms are presented as we know they can be, even in diverse settings and challenging situations. In looking at the effective elementary classroom we will examine four key factors: physical features, materials, organization, and climate.

CAN YOU?

1. Enumerate the essential physical characteristics and material needs of a classroom where language arts instruction is effective?

2. Explain the difference between allocated time and engaged time?

3. Identify and discuss the disadvantages of ability grouping?

4. Describe an ideal "climate" for language arts learning?

5. Explain what is meant by "direct" and "indirect" instruction and give an example of each?

PHYSICAL FEATURES

The size, condition, and shape of classrooms varies considerably from school to school. These physical constraints inevitably affect organization and management of materials and curriculum; however, creative teachers find that the physical features that are most conducive to language learning can be provided in almost any classroom. Whatever the furniture in the room (tables, desks, bulletin boards, shelves, dividers, chairs) it must be flexibly arranged to accommodate different kinds of student grouping. There should be spaces for pairs or small groups of students to work collaboratively and areas that are designed for independent work, for uninterrupted concentration on reading or writing. Large- and small-group instruction must also be provided for through flexible arrangement of tables or desks or by a fairly large carpeted space where children can gather together. In small or crowded classrooms these elements will not all be accessible at the same time, but the teacher needs to plan the physical layout of the room in such a way that furniture can be moved easily and efficiently to create the necessary spaces for different instructional needs. Figure 3-1 shows a diagram of Mr. Benoit's first-grade classroom, described in chapter 1.

Language arts teachers agree on the need for several special areas within the classroom. Perhaps the most important is the classroom library. The books that are present and the way they are arranged and displayed in the classroom reflect the teacher's beliefs about books and reading. The classroom library makes books immediately accessible to students. Research has shown that children who have access to literature collections in their classrooms read significantly more often than children who do not have classroom-housed collections of books (Coody, 1973; Huck, Hepler, and Hickman, 1987).

Another important feature of language-rich classrooms for young children is space for dramatic expression and play. As we shall see, story creation and the retelling of stories that have been heard or read are vital stimulants both to oral language development and to literacy learning.

A third physical feature that language arts teachers find necessary is a special location for keeping student work. Folders, boxes,

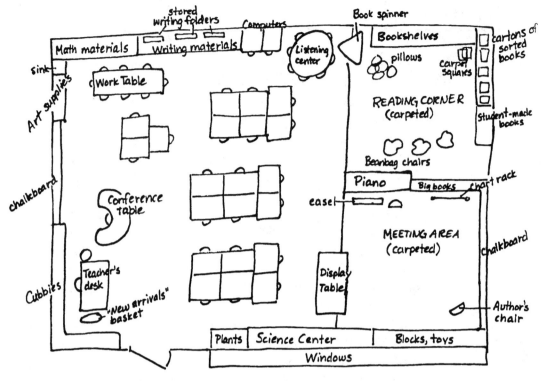

Figure 3-1
Louis Benoit's First-Grade Classroom

drawers, plastic tubs or other containers may be used for this purpose. A particular place in the room is allocated for their storage. Children not only gain a sense of ownership and organization from such an arrangement, they also get the message that their work is important, is valuable enough to save and possibly return to for further revision or evaluation. The privacy of each person's work is respected, and the work is accessible to the students, acknowledging their ownership (Teale, 1989).

MATERIALS

The choice of materials to include in the elementary classroom should be based on the characteristics of the students who will use them. Materials used in language arts instruction must be developmentally appropriate and reflect the range of the children's language proficiencies and interests. Mr. Benoit's classroom library, for example, contains many many short, predictable texts with interesting illustrations, since the majority of his first-graders are initial readers. His collection also includes wordless picture books, nursery rhymes, longer stories, and some chapter books. Fiction, nonfiction, and poetry are all represented. He makes sure he has books that will appeal to the diverse interests and needs of his students.

According to the participants in the 1987 Coalition of English Associations conference, a classroom library that celebrates the diverse backgrounds and interests of children includes

- A generous ratio of books to students. (A *minimum* of three to five

    books per student is recommended. Many would argue that this is too few.)

- Trade books representing a variety of genres, areas of interest, and degrees of complexity. (It is extremely important to include nonfiction texts along with stories.)

- Books authored by children

- Magazines and other periodicals

- Book-related environmental print such as signs, labels, stickers, book covers,and posters (Teale, 1989, pp. 18–19)

Writing materials are another essential ingredient of elementary classrooms that promote the language arts. Writing will be a far more interesting and appealing activity to children if the writing materials and media in the classroom represent, to some extent, the diversity of writing materials and media that exists in the outside world where children encounter bumper stickers, billboards, labels, menus, note pads, birthday cards, diaries, posters, multicolored pens, and computers. The following basic writing materials should be present and accessible to young language learners:

- A variety of kinds of paper of various sizes, shapes, textures, and colors. Lined and unlined paper, "story paper" for primary-grade students (the upper half unlined for drawing, the lower half lined for print), and stapled booklets of blank paper should also be available.

- A variety of writing implements, including pencils, pens, crayons, felt-tip markers, and, if possible, a typewriter or word processor

- Basic spelling and vocabulary resources, such as dictionaries, a thesaurus, word lists, and spelling checkers

- Supplementary writers' tools, including scissors, erasers, white-out, tape, staples, and paste

- Folders for children's writing (one for each child) and materials for simple "publishing" of student works, such as posterboard for book covers, bookbinding tape, contact paper, and a long-arm stapler

To the extent that the school budget allows, it is beneficial to provide children with experiences with electronic expressive media such as tape recorders, record players, cameras, camcorders, and computers.

Another type of materials that enhances language learning in elementary classrooms includes those that are used in dramatic expression and play. Dramatic play, such as playing "house" or "store" in the earliest grades, stimulates oral language development as children rehearse adult roles. If "print props" such as appointment books, tickets, and note pads for lists are available, literacy concepts will develop as well. In the primary and upper elementary grades, literacy and oral language skills are practiced simultaneously as children retell and dramatize stories they have read or had read to them. They need puppets, masks, and simple props, or the materials to make these things.

Children need opportunities to compose and create with artistic media as a complement to or stimulus for language activities. To serve this purpose, the classroom materials should include graphic media such as colored chalk, watercolors or tempera paints, clay, and computer graphics, as well as simple musical instruments.

Finally, a stimulating environment for children includes animals, plants, and objects. While it is wonderful, when possible, to have a resident rabbit or a terrarium in the classroom, there are many other options as well. Artifacts, collections (of rocks, shells, leaves), preserved animals or plants, models, and tools for observation (magnifying glasses, microscopes, thermometers) also stimulate exploration of the environment and language of a special kind: the language of observation, explanation, comparison, and reasoning. We tend to label these materials and their use as parts of the science curriculum. They are nevertheless crucial to language learning.

ORGANIZATION

The organization of the classroom profoundly affects students' learning and their attitudes toward learning. We are not referring here to the physical organization—the room plan or the way the furniture is arranged—but rather to the way in which instruction is organized. Two aspects of instructional organization are particularly important: allotment of time and the grouping of students.

Allotment of Time for Language Arts Instruction

In an effective elementary classroom, children are engaged in speaking and listening throughout the day. Adequate time for engagement in reading and writing must be planned for more specifically. Extended blocks of uninterrupted time for literacy activities are essential. How much time is "adequate"? Typically a total of 1½ to 2 hours devoted to sustained reading and writing activities is recommended as a minimum. (This is referred to as *allocated time*.) In addition, of course, reading and writing are woven into other subject areas.

In the mid-eighties a national task force studied reading instructional practices in classrooms across America. Their findings and recommendations were published in a report entitled *Becoming a Nation of Readers*. One of their most disturbing findings was that children in many classrooms were spending a great deal of time completing worksheets and doing skill exercises, and very little time in sustained reading (Anderson et al., 1985). This situation must change if we are to attain the goal of producing literate students who are active users of their literacy skills throughout their lives.

The time of day at which sustained reading and writing times are scheduled is not as important as the regularity of scheduling. A well-established routine leads students to expect that they will read and write extensively every day.

This policy of adequate time allotment for language arts is easier to state or intend than it is to implement. Today's teachers are asked to attend to so many curricular areas and extra-curricular tasks that finding a consistent, uninterrupted time for reading and writing with all students present in the classroom may prove to be a major challenge. It is a challenge that must be met, however, if our students are to emerge from their school years as readers and writers. Whatever else "gives" in the curriculum, the time for reading and writing is of the highest priority and remains non-negotiable for teachers with truly effective language arts programs.

Important as allocated time is, *engaged time*, or time during which the students are actually reading or writing (not getting materials together, sharpening pencils, or arguing about where to sit) is still more important. Of course the amount of allocated time influences the amount of engaged time, but the skill of the teacher in managing the class is also a major determinant. Effective teachers spend time the first few weeks of school establishing routines with the students for distributing and collecting materials, making transitions between activities, and getting help when the teacher is busy or unavailable. Well-established routines help eliminate wasted time; they also help to prevent discipline problems. When such problems do arise, effective teachers handle them quickly, firmly, and consistently (Brophy, 1983). As skilled managers, teachers are responsible for ensuring that sufficient time is available for students' language activities and that this time is used as productively as possible.

Grouping for Language Arts Instruction

In the classrooms of yesteryear, children were most often grouped according to their ability or achievement levels for reading instruction (typically from a basal reader) and received whole-group instruction in the other language arts areas. Today's teachers tend to use more options for grouping students. They may choose to instruct a large group (whole class), small groups, individuals, or pairs of students. Skilled teachers make use of all these forms of grouping within their literacy programs.

If you observe teachers at work in their classrooms, you will find that they group students for one of three reasons: to address common needs efficiently, to accommodate shared interests or experiences, or to ensure exposure to materials that are at an appropriate difficulty level (O'Donnell and Wood, 1992). In the description of Karen Johnson's classroom in chapter 1, we saw examples of each of these. When Karen modeled formulation of good discussion questions and provided guidelines for small group discussions at the beginning of the year, she did so with the entire class, since all children would need these skills to work with each other in small literature groups. A major purpose of these smaller groups was to give students opportunities to share a common reading experience and thereby enlarge their perspective and understanding of the book. The children had the opportunity to see the books and choose which one they wished to work on. (Karen also made recommendations to individual students from time to time.) One reason for this process was to help children learn to match their reading abilities to the books they chose. Another was to allow them to choose a book that appealed to them personally.

Ability grouping (in teacher-assigned groups) is still used in many classrooms where a commercial basal reader program, consisting of graded books of reading selections with accompanying worksheets and teachers' manuals, is the primary vehicle for reading instruction. Discussion of the formation of such groups and their management is beyond the scope of this text, but will be found in texts that focus on reading development and instruction. It should be mentioned, however, that there are many pitfalls associated with ability grouping, including differences in quality and quantity of instruction in "high" and "low" reading groups, the fact that children who are relegated to a "low" group seldom move out of it, and the likelihood that "low" group members will view themselves as inferior to children in the "high" groups (who will agree). In classrooms where teachers do not use or do not adhere closely to a basal reading program, but instead base a great deal of their instruction on the reading of "real" children's books, ability grouping is less frequently used. In any case, it is recommended that teachers explore other options for grouping, such as whole-class instruction, collaborative special interest groups, and work with partners. Children need the experience of working with all their classmates in varied combinations and of feeling like valued contributors to a community of learners (Duffy and Roehler, 1986).

CLIMATE

The overall climate of the classroom is affected by all of the factors already mentioned (physical features, materials, and organization). In addition, the climate is determined by the teacher's attitudes and beliefs about children, about learning and teaching, and about the language arts. These attitudes and beliefs are reflected in teachers' interactions with their students. Current understandings about language learning that influence the climate of today's elementary classrooms include the following:

- Recognition of the importance of Cambourne's conditions for language learning (see chapter 2)

- Recognition that literacy acquisition is a language-learning process and therefore follows the same principles and requires the same conditions as oral language learning

- Recognition that all forms of language learning (including learning to read and write) require social interaction and sharing

- Shift from emphasis on products (in both teaching and assessment) to more emphasis on processes—the strategies of discussing, reading, writing, and problem solving

- Shift from viewing teachers as technicians, dispensers of information, to viewing them as decision-makers, facilitators of learning

These new understandings have led not only to major changes in organization and management of language arts instruction, but also to a classroom climate that is quite different from the climate that prevailed 20 years ago. There has been a subtle but important shift in roles and responsibilities. Teachers who understand and create Cambourne's conditions for language learning in their classrooms are fully in charge of their teaching, but expect students to be responsible for their own learning, and convey this expectation to them. Such teachers provide information, direction, modeling, and response, but they also value students as people and as language learners and help them to plan, question, collaborate, make choices, and monitor their own learning. Language learning inevitably involves risk taking; therefore the teacher must create an atmosphere in which risk taking is not threatening. Children become risk takers only when their attempts and contributions are accepted and valued, and "mistakes" are recognized as an important and natural part of learning.

Today's teacher tries to provide a balance between teacher responsibility and student responsibility. This is reflected in the kinds and proportions of instruction used.

Instruction can be defined as the design and manipulation of experiences by the teacher to enable students to achieve desired curricular outcomes, and it may be either *direct* or *indirect*. In direct instruction the teacher assumes an active, dominant role and provides information the students are presumed to need to achieve desired outcomes. Indirect instruction, in contrast, derives from a structured environment and teacher facilitation, rather than from direction and explanation. Activities are designed in such a way that students are led to discover outcomes for themselves (Duffy and Roehler, 1986). Karen Johnson used direct instruction during the whole-class minilessons she conducted at the beginning of writing workshop time (see chapter 1). When literature groups met in her classroom to formulate their own questions and discuss their reading according to a format she had suggested to them, the instruction that was going on was indirect.

Both direct and indirect instruction have an important place in implementation of the language arts curriculum. The teacher chooses to use one or the other according to the nature of the desired outcomes. The teacher must decide what blend of direct and indirect instruction will be most appropriate for the students. (You will encounter many more examples of both types of instruction in subsequent chapters on oral and written communication.) This blend affects the classroom climate. A teacher who employs direct instruction much or all of the time is likely to create a classroom climate that is very restrictive, where children feel little responsibility for their own learning and undervalued as learners. Language arts instruction particularly lends itself to indirect instruction; nevertheless, if there is insufficient structure and accountability, the climate can become chaotic and less productive than it might be, and children may not get the information and support they need to progress to their full potential. The goal is to create a climate in which individuals can flourish as well as participate as valued members of the group. This requires an environment that is predictable but flexible, stimulating but not chaotic, and disciplined but not restrictive.

LOOKING BACK

The physical features, materials, organization, and overall climate of a classroom influence the effectiveness of language arts instruction. Whatever the space and type of furniture in the room, it is essential that it be movable to accommodate different kinds of student grouping. Special areas of the classroom are also important, most notably an inviting and well-arranged library. Reading and writing materials should be varied and appropriate to the developmental level of the students. Adequate time must be allotted for language arts activities, and we must do everything we can to ensure that children are fully engaged during this time. Various forms of grouping will be used by teachers to accomplish different purposes. Two benchmarks of good grouping practices are emphasis on collaboration between students in group situations and avoidance of overuse of "ability"-based groups. The overall climate of the classroom, which is determined largely by the teacher's attitudes and beliefs about children and learning, has perhaps the most influence on children's learning and their view of themselves as learners.

This chapter's description of important aspects of the elementary classroom has been quite general. In subsequent chapters you will find applications and examples of the ideas presented here.

SELF-TEST

1. Return to the chapter 1 descriptions of the first- and fourth-grade classrooms and examine them from the perspective of what you have learned in chapters 2 and 3. What evidence do you see of Cambourne's conditions for language learning in these settings?

2. How do the two classrooms reflect the recommendations about physical features, materials, organization, and climate?

3. Reflect on classrooms you have been in, as a student or as an observer. Give examples of instances of direct and indirect teaching that occurred.

4. Observe a block of language arts instruction in a classroom. Note the different forms of student grouping used during that time. Try to determine, in each instance, the *basis* and the *rationale* for each particular grouping configuration. Suggest other forms of grouping that might have worked equally well or better for the students involved.

5. In what ways might teachers' knowledge-base influence the classroom climate they create? Give examples.

BIBLIOGRAPHY

Anderson, R.C., Hiebert, E., Scott, J., & Wilkinson, I. (Eds.). (1985). *Becoming a nation of readers.* Washington, D.C.: National Institute of Education.

Brophy, J.E. (1983). Classroom organization and management. *Elementary School Journal, 83,* 265-285.

Coody, B. (1973). *Using literature with young children.* Dubuque, IA.: Brown.

Duffy, G.G. and Roehler, L.R. (1986). *Improving classroom reading instruction.* New York: Random House.

Huck, C., Hepler, S. and Hickman, J. (1987). *Children's literature in the elementary school* (4th ed.). New York: Holt, Rinehart and Winston.

O'Donnell, M. and Wood, M. (1992). *Becoming a reader: a developmental approach to reading instruction.* Boston: Allyn and Bacon.

Teale, W. (1989). Language arts for the 21st century. In Jensen, J. (ed.), *Stories to grow on.* Portsmouth, N.H.: Heinemann.

4 Oral Communication in the Elementary Classroom

LOOKING AHEAD

This chapter is divided into two parts. Part One deals with listening and the promotion of active listening in the classroom. Listening involves receiving incoming messages, attending to them, and constructing meaning from them. As teachers, we can facilitate students' listening by encouraging participation and responses to what they hear. Various purposes for listening may be delineated, although they often overlap. We can ensure that our students experience appreciative, informational, and critical listening and that they learn to give appropriate responses.

Part Two focuses on the uses of talk in the classroom. Our goals for students include the development of conversational skills and the use of appropriate linguistic and social conventions. Informal conversations, teacher- or student-led discussions, and formal oral presentations, all contribute to becoming an effective user of language. Oral language plays unique roles in literature study and in the content areas of science and social studies. These are areas of the curriculum in which teachers can be particularly effective in promoting oral language growth.

CAN YOU?

1. Explain how listening is different from hearing?

2. List several ways in which teachers help students to attend and to assign meaning when they listen?

3. Specify important goals for students in language use, thinking patterns, and interpersonal functioning?

4. Explain the importance of story retelling in the early grades?

5. Explain the importance of discussing a topic before reading about it?

PART ONE: PROMOTING ACTIVE LISTENING

Listening is the foundational language mode in that it provides the basis for learning to speak, read, and write. Children construct their knowledge and use of oral language by listening to the speech of those around them. They are introduced to reading by listening to stories read aloud to them. As literate caregivers translate print into oral language for them, they begin to make connections between what they hear and what they see on the printed page. Listening is also essential to the writing process as students share their writing in conferences and receive feedback. Writing also involves "inner listening," or dialoguing with the self, particularly when revising. Both school children and adults spend more time in listening than in reading, writing, and talking combined. In the words of researcher Jane Hansen, "A writing/reading program begins with listening, and listening holds the program together" (1987, p. 69).

RECEIVING, ATTENDING, AND ASSIGNING MEANING

Exactly what do we mean by "listening?" *Listening* is not simply a synonym for *hearing*. Hearing is certainly an integral component of listening, but it must be followed by the construction of meaning from what is heard. Listening is a complex process in which the mind converts spoken language to meaning. There are actually three parts to this process: *receiving, attending,* and *assigning meaning* (Wolvin and Coakley, 1979). In receiving speech, the listener hears, or takes in, the aural stimuli presented by the speaker. (In the case of sign language exchanges, the receiver takes in the visual stimuli provided by the signer.) Attending, or "paying attention," to use the term teachers most often employ, involves focusing on the important information in the message while ignoring irrelevant or distracting stimuli. The extent to which the listener attends depends greatly on motivation and interest in the message, as well as on the presence or absence of significant distractions in the environment. In assigning meaning, or understanding the message, the listener fits the information in the message into his or her existing conceptual framework. The extent to which the listener understands the message is largely dependent upon prior knowledge (knowledge of the concepts and vocabulary used by the speaker) and upon the clarity of the message. For example, if your science lab instructor directs you to "Pour the chlorine solution from the third beaker into three test tubes," you may hear, attending to the message with great concentration, but if you do not already know the meanings of the terms *beaker, solution,* and *test tube,* you will not understand well enough to carry out the instructions without further explanation.

Teachers who understand what is involved in listening can help children learn to attend and to assign meaning more effectively in the following ways.

Attending

- Direct students' attention to the speaker. Do not begin giving directions, reading aloud, or asking questions until all students are quiet and looking at the speaker. Teach children the signals of being "ready to listen": sitting quietly without talking, eyes on the speaker, hands empty. In other words, anticipate and minimize possible distractions. Expect students' full attention; wait for them to give it. Do this consistently, every time it is necessary for the group to listen.

- Discuss with students the purpose for the listening they are about to engage in and let them know what kind of response will be expected of them.

- Use cues, when speaking, to let listeners know what is most important for them to attend to. Such cues include voice inflections and emphasis, important points jotted on the blackboard, explicit statements such as, "This is especially important." Discuss these cues with children so they are aware of speakers' intent in using them.

Assigning Meaning

- Make sure listeners have adequate prior knowledge to make sense of what they will hear. Assess their experience with important concepts through questioning and discussion. Build unfamiliar concepts through direct or vicarious experiences.

- Have students predict what the message or story will contain. This helps them listen purposefully as they check what they hear against their predictions.

- Use visual aids such as pictures or diagrams to clarify the message when appropriate. Children can also be encouraged to use imagery, that is, to form pictures in their minds based on what they are hearing, especially when listening for enjoyment.

- Check students' understanding of the message by having them briefly summarize, react, or explain.

PARTICIPATION AND RESPONSE

Realistically, listening is inextricably combined with responding. Listening is more effective when it is one part of a two-part communication process. In *conversational* listening/speaking situations or face-to-face discussions, listener and speaker take turns; there is frequent role shifting from speaker to listener and back again. Good examples of this in the classroom setting are writing conferences between pairs of children and small group discussions of literature. In *presentational* situations, one person or several people take the role of speaker, and the listeners become an audience. Examples of presentations would include Louis Benoit reading aloud to his first-graders and one of the literacy groups in Karen Johnson's class presenting their literature response project to their peers.

Listening tends to be more active and sustained when the listener is called on to participate or respond, even in presentational situations. When Mr. Benoit reads a book aloud to his class, he pauses frequently, inviting children to comment and to predict what will come next. When Ms. Johnson gives directions to her class, she often asks the children to turn to a partner and explain the directions, thus making sure everyone understands. Good teachers keep their students engaged as listeners by inviting participation and expecting responses.

Most texts list three kinds of listening which involve different purposes: *appreciative* listening, for enjoyment of what is heard; *informational* listening, in which the listener is gathering information; and *critical* listening, in order to analyze or evaluate what is heard. Although it may be useful for you to be aware of these classifications, in real listening situations you will often find that more than one of these purposes is involved. When Mr. Benoit reads Maurice Sendak's *There's a Nightmare in My Closet,* his students are engaged primarily in appreciative listening. When he reads them Tomie dePaola's *The Cloud Book*, their listening is both appreciative and informational. After reading Roald Dahl's *James and the Giant Peach* to her class for their enjoyment, Karen Johnson reread descriptions of Aunt Spiker and Aunt Sponge while her students listened to determine what techniques the author had used to produce effective character descriptions. They listened both appreciatively and critically, and analyzed Dahl's writing to add some of his techniques to their own repertoires as writers.

Teachers often give special attention to critical listening and thinking activities, since children of all ages are subjected to many kinds of persuasion and propaganda. There is peer pressure to dress and talk as friends do. They see films and hear speakers on issues such as pollution, nuclear power, and drugs. They are exposed to television commercials that are specifically directed at children. It is essential that they learn to listen critically to recognize the techniques of persuasion and the propaganda devices used by advertisers, and to judge their claims.

Marie LaChance, a fifth-grade teacher, introduces her students to the following propaganda devices, eliciting examples from the children:

> *Testimonials*—An advertiser employs a famous athlete or TV star to endorse a product. The message is, "So and So uses this product. If you use it you will be more like So and So. It must be good if So and So says it is."
>
> *Card Stacking*—The persuader presents only one side of an issue or product. Unfavorable aspects or facts are suppressed. To con-

sider the argument or product objectively, the listener must seek further information and alternative viewpoints. For example, many children have acquired toys that were made to sound very appealing in an advertisement, only to find that they were not well made and broke easily.

Bandwagon—An advertiser claims that everyone (or everyone in a prestigious group) is using this product; therefore you should, too. For example, "More doctors use this pain killer than any other." The listener is not told just what "any other" refers to or what "more doctors" means.

Rewards—Sometimes advertisers offer rewards for buying their products. There is a toy in the cereal; if you buy two pairs of shoes you get the second pair at half price; the fast food restaurant will give you a free glass with every order. Listeners should consider the value of the reward and whether it has actually increased the cost of the product. Do they need the product anyway, or are they just attracted by the reward?

Deceptive Language—Misleading language may be used. Beware of phrases such as "new improved," "all natural," "light," or "25% better." This sort of language is misleading because it gives incomplete information. "Better" than what? What is meant by "natural" or "light"?

When Ms. LaChance's students have identified examples of each of these advertising ploys, she asks them to go home and listen critically to advertisements on television and try to identify the propaganda techniques being used by the advertisers. The students jot down examples and bring them to class for discussion. Later on, she has them work in collaborative groups to create advertisements using the techniques they have studied. They "broadcast" their ads to their classmates, who then identify the propaganda devices used and ask appropriate questions about the products.

Over the next few weeks, the fifth-graders note advertisements and commercials that they believe are misleading or deceptive. They write letters of complaint to watchdog agencies. Ms. LaChance uses this opportunity to review letter-writing format, and she helps the students edit their letters, making sure they have described the ad, told where and when they saw or heard it, and explained what they found offensive about it. Agencies children may write to include

Action for Children's Television
46 Austin St.
Newton, MA 02160

Children's Advertising Review Unit
Council of Better Business Bureaus
845 Third Ave.
New York, NY 10022

Federal Trade Commission
Pennsylvania Ave. at Sixth St. NW
Washington, DC 20580

Zillions Ad Complaints
256 Washington St.
Mt. Vernon, NY 10553

PART TWO: TALK IN THE CLASSROOM

Talk is the most frequently used expressive language mode. Most children are fluent users of oral language by the time they start school. Since children have already acquired considerable competence in using oral language, teachers often assume that talk does not need to be emphasized in elementary classrooms. (In fact, teachers generally spend considerable effort preventing children from talking and controlling their talk.) Research has shown us, however, that students benefit greatly from participation in both informal and formal talk activities. Oral language is an essential ingredient of learning (Cazden, 1986). Elementary school children tell, retell, and discuss stories they have read or heard. They converse with peers as they plan and carry out collaborative projects or conduct writing conferences. They give oral reports in science or social studies to share their learning with others.

GOALS FOR STUDENTS

What are the conversational skills and conventions (both linguistic and social) that we wish to help children acquire during their elementary school years? Hennings (1990) delineates them as follows:

Conversational skills are of several types. A first series of skills to be achieved through classroom interaction relates to language use. The conversationalist is able to

1. Select the appropriate words to communicate ideas clearly;

2. Use sentence patterns that make his or her ideas easy to follow;

3. Shift from formal to informal language patterns depending on the situation.

A second series of skills relates to thinking patterns. The conversationalist is able to

1. Follow the line of thought of previous speakers and comment and ask questions in terms of what has gone before;

2. Put thoughts together in a logical and clear way;

3. See the relationships between the major ideas being discussed and specific information he or she can contribute;

4. Move the conversation forward by generalizing, summarizing, or hypothesizing.

A third series relates to interpersonal functioning. The conversationalist is able to

1. Wait his or her turn to comment and not monopolize the conversation;

2. Encourage others to comment or raise questions;

3. Contribute with confidence and poise;

4. Contribute courteously with control over voice and body (p. 178).

CONVERSING

Teachers of primary-grade children usually encourage informal conversation by setting up areas in the classroom where children can engage in cooperative play or exploration. For example, the classroom may contain a block building area, a science corner with interesting materials to examine and a pet to observe and care for, or a play store constructed from large cardboard cartons. In addition to the spontaneous social interactions that occur in the classroom and on the playground, meaningful conversation between children is stimulated by an interesting environment provided by the teacher. The resulting abundance of informal, social language exchanges leads to the enhancement of the first three conversational skills mentioned by Hennings.

DISCUSSING

As children advance through the elementary grades, teachers tend to focus less on informal conversations and more on discussions, which are more structured. Discussions are the chief means by which the conversational skills related to thinking patterns and to interpersonal functioning are developed. During the early elementary years, these skills are taught largely through teacher modeling. The teacher must contribute as well as solicit comments related to the topic under discussion, verbalize connections among ideas being discussed, and demonstrate the processes of hypothesizing, summarizing, and generalizing. Gradually students incorporate these conversation skills into their own discussions. The example that follows is from Thom Wendt's mixed fourth/fifth-grade classroom:

Following the sharing of a book about carnivorous plants, Todd and Steve found some information about a species of wasp that lays its eggs in pitcher plants. They were eager to share their information with their classmates. They explained the process the parent wasp goes through in preparing the egg nests.

Bobby raised his hand to ask, "Don't the pitcher plants eat the wasps and eggs inside the plant?"

"That's a real good question," Todd remarked with a look of puzzlement in Steve's direction.

"Didn't it say someplace that they only lay their eggs in last year's pitchers?" Steve asked. Both boys looked through the pages as we waited in anticipation. "Yes, they only build a nest in the dead parts from last season."

"Well, that makes sense," Bobby said. "That way the plant wouldn't be able to eat the baby wasps." (Wendt, 1990)

Note that in this brief discussion, the children employed all four of Hennings' skills related to thinking patterns. They stuck to the topic, raised related questions, hypothesized, and drew conclusions. In observing classroom discussions you will undoubtedly notice that when children are truly interested and engaged in the subject they are discussing, the elements of good discussion are more likely to be incorporated by the children.

OBSERVING SOCIAL CONVENTIONS

The third series of skills specified by Hennings relates to courtesy. Respect for others involved in the oral interaction is important and is not easy to teach, since each child's self-concept and value system affects interactions. Once again, the best place for a teacher to start is by serving as a model of courteous communication. Joan Whiteside, a kindergarten teacher, makes a point of modeling politeness and thoughtfulness in her interactions with her young students. When she has to stop in the middle of reading to the children to attend to a message from the office, she says, "Excuse me for just a moment, boys and girls." When several children help pick up the felt-tip markers that have been spilled from their can, she thanks them for their help. When a visitor arrives in the classroom, she gets the children's attention and introduces the newcomer by name. She invites the children to welcome the visitor by saying, "Good morning" or "Hello." She also explains the purposes for social conventions when the opportunity arises. " Billy, we want to be fair and give everyone a turn to talk. You already had a turn, so you need to wait until everyone else has had their chance." Later she compliments the group for giving everyone a turn. When she sees two children sitting very close together and pushing at one another, she says to the group, "Sasha and Andrea don't have enough room to be comfortable. Let's all move over just a bit to give them more room." Not only does Ms. Whiteside's politeness set the tone for her students, it helps her maintain discipline. Children are likely to model their conversation and behavior after a teacher who clearly respects them and whom they respect. For older children, it is helpful to discuss the rules of courteous interactions and to generate and post a short list of important behaviors to observe in conversations and discussions. This kind of explicit instruction is unlikely to be effective, however, if the teacher fails to model the behaviors and to insist that students observe them consistently.

Talk, then, serves both social and learning functions; it has a valid place in the language curriculum. Teachers must plan opportunities for talk and incorporate them into the curriculum in such a way that children will use talk productively for a variety of purposes. In the discussion that follows, we will focus first on talk related to literature experiences (particularly stories), then on the use of talk in content-area learning, and finally on teacher guidelines for promoting oral language growth.

ORAL LANGUAGE AND LITERATURE

Listening to stories told or read aloud has been emphasized as an essential contributor to language and literacy learning. Just hearing or reading literature is not enough, however. Elementary school youngsters should have daily opportunities to participate in literature reading or telling and to respond orally and creatively to their literacy experiences. They participate in the literacy experience when they *predict* what will happen, *read along* with the teacher from enlarged texts, *fill in* words or phrases when the story reader pauses, and *comment* on or *ask questions* about the text. Ways to respond orally and creatively to stories usually involve story *retelling*, often with the aid of puppets, illustrations, or props. These activities are not extras or "frills" in the language arts program; they are essential because they lead to increased comprehension and heightened ability to use both oral and written language.

Story Retelling

The oral retelling of stories in a variety of ways is an especially important activity for primary-grade children. Retelling activities help children assimilate story language and become increasingly aware of story structure and sequence (Gambrell, Pfeiffer, and Wilson, 1985). Through many opportunities to retell stories, young children learn to start by introducing characters and setting, go on to explain the central problem or theme, mention plot episodes in order, and describe the resolution. In other words, they demonstrate the ability to organize the story coherently (O'Donnell and Wood, 1992). Compare these two retellings of Maurice Sendak's *Where the Wild Things Are* by a kindergarten child who lacked extensive literacy experiences and by a first-grader who had had many experiences with stories, both at home and in school.

Retelling by Cory, in October of his kindergarten year:

> The boy put on his, um, fox suit. And he was bad. So he went in his room, and he went in the woods. He saw lots of aminals (sic).

Retelling by Mario, in April of his first-grade year:

> It was about Max. He was a little boy and he liked to play wild. One night he put on his wolf suit and he made lots of mischief. So his mother made him go in his room and not have any supper. When Max was in his room he thought a forest was growing in his room and the walls were trees and they were all around him. There was an ocean too, and a boat that Max could get into and sail away. And he sailed all the way to the land where the wild things lived. They were scary! They gnashed their terrible teeth and roared their terrible roars. But Max was brave, so they didn't hurt him. He yelled at them, "STOP!" and he stared right at their yellow eyes. They stopped acting so scary, and they made him the king of all of them. He said, "Let the wild rumpus start." And they all danced around and swung off the trees and acted wild and crazy. But after awhile, Max got tired of it, and he sat down and looked sad, because he was lonely and he missed his family. So he got in the boat to go home. The wild things didn't want him to go, and they told him they would eat him up, but he said "No," and sailed away anyway. He went all the way back in and out of weeks and days all the way back to his room. And when he finally got there, he found his supper and it was still hot.

Clearly Mario's retelling of the story is far more complete than Cory's. Mario described all the important events of the story in the correct sequence, included many details, and incorporated language from the story ("they gnashed their terrible teeth").

Teachers can help children develop retelling ability through structured discussions of stories read aloud that follow the usual story pattern. The teacher actually leads children through a simple reconstruction of the story using a series of prompts such as the following:

- Who was the story about?

- How did the story begin?

- What was _____'s problem? Or, what did _____ want to do?

- What happened?

- What happened next?

- Was _____ able to solve his problem?

- How did the story end? (O'Donnell and Wood, 1992, p. 20.)

While recapitulation of stories is useful in helping young children learn to retell stories more completely, it is important not to limit story discussions to this purpose and format. Even the youngest children should be encouraged to interpret, compare characters, and link stories to other stories or to their own life experiences. Various props may be used to stimulate creative retelling and interpretation of stories.

Storyboards, for example, are easy to construct and to use for retelling. Storyboards generally consist of a piece of cardboard or oaktag on which key elements of the story setting are represented. A first-grader's storyboard for *The Three Billy Goats Gruff* would probably include a bridge, hills, grass, and perhaps water under the bridge, all cut from colored construction paper and glued on the oaktag background. Parts of the scene can be painted with watercolors or colored with crayons. Primary-grade teachers often construct one or two simple storyboards, discussing with the children how they decided what to include and how they proceeded to make the board. Once the making of a storyboard has been demonstrated, children enjoy making their own. Oaktag cutouts of the major story characters (which may be attached to popsicle sticks to make stick puppets) are stored in a construction paper pocket stapled to the back of the storyboard. Primary-grade children should be given many opportunities to use the storyboards, alone (for rehearsal) or with other children to repeatedly recreate their favorite stories. Nina

Jones, a kindergarten teacher, keeps a set of ten storyboards that she has made at school for children to use. She encourages them to take home the storyboards they make themselves and retell the stories to family members or other caregivers.

Puppets are another type of prop that is particularly appropriate for young children to use. Puppets lend themselves particularly well to the retelling of stories that contain a lot of dialogue. Stick puppets, finger puppets, and paper bag puppets, as well as other kinds, can be simply made from readily available materials. Stuffed animals and small dolls can also be used to represent characters. Virtually all children enjoy using puppets, and their use often enables shy children to feel more comfortable retelling stories. (See appendix A for descriptions of easy-to-make puppets.)

Drama, or acting out a story, with or without props is another way to retell. Young children can plan and carry out improvised re-enactments of stories informally. A stage, a script, and elaborate costumes and scenery are not necessary. Primary-grade children enjoy putting on impromptu dramatizations of stories for their classmates. Simple props are helpful, but much is left to the imagination. Chalk lines on the floor designate a road, chairs become trees, or desks are rearranged to represent a house. Nina Jones keeps a box of costume props in her classroom. The items in it include several shawls and scarves of different colors that can be easily draped over a child to form a cloak, a skirt, or a kerchief, several hats, a "magic wand," and long ears and tails made of oaktag that can be taped or pinned to headbands or belts.

Many teachers of primary-grade children report that adult supervision is necessary when groups of children create dramatizations, since a high degree of cooperation is necessary. The teacher or an aide or volunteer helps the children decide fairly who will play which role and what events to include, and guides them through a practice run or two. Dramatizing stories is an activity that most children enjoy immensely; however it requires more sustained time and effort by children and teacher than some of the other retelling activities.

Story retelling should not end with the primary grades. Upper-grade elementary students continue to profit from retelling activities, although of course the form of the activities will reflect their greater maturity and skill. Puppet shows and dramatizations of stories they have read can become more elaborate in grades four through eight. Students are better able to sustain a project over a period of time. They can create more sophisticated puppets, make scenery, write and memorize scripts, and rehearse their dramatizations. They can retell stories in writing and then share and compare their retellings (Cambourne, 1990). They can give booktalks, in which they highlight characters, main events, and theme of a book for their classmates. As always, new forms of retelling or responding to literature must be modeled by the teacher, and students must be guided through each new process. Remember that the time and effort that goes into retelling activities is time well spent. These activities lead students to sequence stories, analyze characters in order to portray them, work with the structure of stories, expand vocabulary, remember and use story language, and speak to an audience.

Discussions about Literature

Discussions often follow the reading aloud of a book or the completion of books students have read on their own. Teachers make particularly extensive use of discussions in the middle and upper elementary grades when most children are reading chapter books. Whether the teacher is conversing with one student in an individual reading conference, with a small group, or with the entire class, it is important to remember that the purpose of the discussion is to stimulate deeper understanding and appreciation of the text and to explore students' responses to it, rather than to check their comprehension. Higgins (quoted in Eeds and Wells, 1989) reminds us, "What you often get are gentle inquisitions, when what you really want are grand conversations" (p. 4). The teacher who wishes to facilitate "grand conversations" must take part in discussions in order to learn rather than to judge. From students' responses we learn what they are thinking, what they value, what moves them, what they like and dislike, and what they understand from their own perspectives. Most of the questions asked do not have predetermined "right" answers. Students are encouraged to reflect on their reading, both critically and creatively, in the context of their life (and literature) experiences. In a successful literature discussion, the group becomes a community of learners sharing personal responses to literature and enhancing and extending everyone's understanding.

ORAL LANGUAGE AND LEARNING IN THE CONTENT AREAS

Content-area study provides rich opportunities for the use of oral language to enhance learning. Unfortunately research indicates that much of the verbal interaction that occurs in elementary classrooms requires students only to give one-word or short-phrase answers to teachers' questions. Teachers do most of the explaining and talking, and little dialoguing between students occurs (DeStephano, Pepinsky, and Sanders, 1982). We need to identify ways in which children can use a range of diverse language functions (see chapter 2), as they do outside of school, to become more effective users of language and to reflect on their experiences.

Discussions (Conversing)

When are discussions likely to occur in connection with content-area study? Novice teachers often assume that discussion takes place after students have taken in new information through reading their texts, watching a film, or hearing a speaker. We now know, however, that the discussion that takes place *before* exposure to new information is vitally important in promoting students' understanding of the new material. Comprehension builds largely on prior knowledge. In order to understand, students must make connections between the new information and what they already know based on their experiences. Therefore it is essential for the teacher to find out, through discussion, what students already know about the topic under consideration, to assess their prior knowledge. If the students are extremely unfamiliar with major concepts that they are going to encounter in their reading or listening, the teacher must provide them with some experiences that build the necessary background knowledge. Through discussion, students and teacher share knowledge. In addition, the teacher helps students speculate about what they will read or hear about. They form predictions and set purposes for listening or reading. These steps are important in facilitating comprehension of the new material. Following are excerpts from a discussion that took place in George Delaney's fourth-grade classroom before the children read a selection in their science book about tornadoes. The school in which Mr. Delaney teaches is located on the coast of Maine. All of the children had had direct experience with hurricanes, but their teacher assumed they knew much less about tornadoes, which do occur in that part of the country, but rarely.

Mr. D.: Yesterday we learned a lot about hurricanes. Today we will learn about another kind of storm, tornadoes. Who has heard of tornadoes? [Most of the third graders raised their hands.] Where have you heard about them; what are they like?

Susan: We lived in Texas when I was a baby. My mom said there was a special part of the cellar to hide in if they thought a tornado was coming, because it could pick houses right up, and cars, and smash everything.

Mr. D.: Yes, tornadoes can do a lot of damage.

Andy: There was a tornado in *The Wizard of Oz.*

Ricardo: Oh yeah! I saw that on TV, and my sister has the book.

Mr. D.: You're right. A tornado was a very important part of that story. Does anyone know how a tornado is different from a hurricane?

Susan: It's different. It's more scary because you don't have any warning. Like before the hurricane they had it on TV all day, so people could get ready.

Mr. D.: So you think tornadoes strike more suddenly?

Susan: Yes.

Ben: They're bigger. They're all black.

Anna: We don't have them in Maine, do we?

Angela: Oh yes! Yes, we do. My cousin lives in Richmond, and they had one there and her friend's trailer got picked right up and smashed. But they weren't home. My cousin said it was all in one place. She didn't have it at her house.

Mr. D.: Well, that must mean that it's *not* as big as a hurricane. It affects a smaller area. O.K., you know some things about tornadoes, but we need to find out more. I brought in some pictures to show you.

Mr. D. showed the children photographs of approaching tornadoes which he had clipped from a magazine and saved. The students noted the funnel shape, and he mentioned that tornadoes are often called "twisters." The children noticed that the background in the pictures was flat prairie land, and he told them that tornadoes most commonly occur in flatlands. After the brief discussion, he asked the students to suggest questions they had about tornadoes. They came up with the following questions, which he recorded on the board:

- Where do they come from? What kind of weather makes them happen?

- Why do they twist and have a funnel shape?

- Why are they more common in the prairies? Why don't we have them very often in Maine?

Mr. Delaney also contributed a question to guide their reading:

- How are tornadoes different from hurricanes?

The students now had some purposes for their reading. They predicted that some, at least, of their questions would be answered in the text. Through discussion, Mr. Delaney had assessed their prior knowledge about tornadoes, provided some background information that most of them seemed to lack, and helped them generate purposes for reading.

After the fourth-graders read the selection on tornadoes, Mr. Delaney referred to the list of questions on the board to guide the discussion. The children talked about the new information. From their comments and questions, Mr. Delaney could see how well they had understood the reading. The last question had not been addressed in the text. Mr. Delaney broke the class into discussion groups and gave them the task of coming up with lists of similarities and differences between the two kinds of storm. Because the students were interested in the topic and had clear directions and a task to accomplish, they worked together well. Each group of four or five students produced a list of similarities and differences, recorded by one of the group members. Under Mr. Delaney's directions they consolidated their lists on two large pieces of paper. Through discussion, the students' understanding of the topic under study had definitely been deepened.

The research on effective questioning during discussions has been reviewed by Wilen (1986), who came up with these suggestions:

- Ask carefully planned questions to organize and direct the lesson.

- Ask single questions that are clearly phrased, rather than vaguely worded or multiple questions.

- Ask questions in a planned sequence.

- Ask factual questions to check basic understanding, but focus on higher-level questions that give students opportunities to think critically and creatively.

- Ask questions to follow up students' responses.

- Give students sufficient time to think about questions and plan their responses.

- Encourage wide participation through interaction among students, drawing in non-volunteers, and seating students in a circle.

- Promote student involvement by having students create questions to ask, lead the discussion, and follow up ideas developed during the discussion.

Oral Reports (Presenting)

The very mention of oral reports brings back unpleasant memories for many of us. We recall being assigned a topic, laboring over the gathering of information (most often copied from an encyclopedia), standing alone in front of our fidgeting peers, feeling self-conscious, embarrassed, and scared, reading our notes verbatim with an occasional glance at the audience, and all the while the teacher sat in the back of the room marking a checklist, judging our performance, and assigning a grade. If we learned anything from such experiences, it was to dread public speaking.

Learning to prepare and deliver oral reports is an important part of the curriculum, particularly for middle- and upper-grade students. It can be a positive, confidence-building experience if real purposes are honored and adequate guidance in the process is provided. First, we must remember (and convey to students) that research reports serve genuine language functions—to inform or (less frequently) to persuade. When students give reports, they learn in-depth about the chosen topic and develop their communication abilities. Teachers must guide inexperienced students through the four steps in preparing reports: choosing a topic, gathering information, organizing the information, and making the presentation.

Students need to be involved in *choosing a topic*. If topics are arbitrarily assigned by the teacher, students feel no ownership and tend to invest less effort and energy in preparing the report. Sometimes the teacher limits students to a broad topic within an area of class study, but has them choose their specific topics. For example, third-grade teacher Kathy O'Dell, whose students were engaged in studying the human body, asked each student to select a different part of the body to report on. Because all of them would be reporting on body parts, the class as a whole was able to determine (with guidance from the teacher) several key points that would be included in all reports: description of the body part, where it is located in the body, what function it performs, and other interesting information. A sixth-grade teacher whose class is studying the Middle Ages might give her students a broader choice of topics, such as any aspect of medieval life. In this case, students' key points would be different and would have to be developed by each individual. Regardless of how broad or limited the choice is, students need to consider what they know about their topic and what they need to learn about it and include in their report.

One useful strategy for planning the research is to create a cluster (sometimes referred to as a *semantic map* or *web*), with the topic at the center, circled, and key ideas recorded at the ends of lines radiating out from the central topic. Kathy O'Dell, whose students were studying the human body, shared the cluster depicted in figure 4-1 with her students.

She then erased "Body Part" from the central circle and wrote in "Lungs." She proceeded to add information to the "spokes" of her cluster (Figure 4.2). As she did this, she used an effective teaching technique called *think aloud*, verbalizing the train of thought that led to her actions.

Let's see, now, how would I describe the lungs? They're in the chest, one on each side, so I'll put that up here, for "where it's located." For structure, I think I'll include what they are made of,

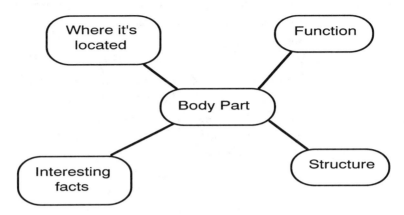

Figure 4-1
Cluster Diagram: Body Parts

many, many tiny air sacs. I think they're about as big as fists, but I'm not sure, so I'll put a question mark. Maybe when I read about them I'll find out. I'll probably add some more parts of the description after I learn more. Now, let's see...function. What do the lungs do?

She proceeded in this manner with every part of the cluster.

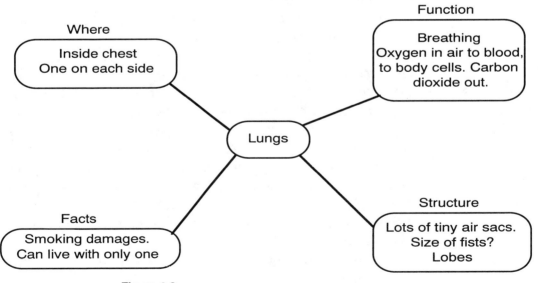

Figure 4-2
Cluster Diagram: Lungs

Another technique that students can use in planning is generating questions they hope to answer through their research. Jamie, one of the sixth-graders who was studying the Middle Ages, came up with the following questions to guide his report on the lives of peasants:

What were their houses like?

Were they different in different places and at different times?

Did peasents have any legal rights?

What was their food like?

How did they get what they needed?

Did they have money? Trade? Depend on the feudal lords for everything?

If someone was born in a peasant family, would they always be a peasant?

What were the biggest problems for the peasants?

Jamie generated the original list of questions and revised it based on input from his teacher and several of his peers before he began his research. Activities such as making a cluster or generating a list of questions help students to narrow their topics and set purposes for their research. Of course new key ideas may be discovered and added or used to replace some of those originally included; however, the process of considering, organizing, and planning tentatively is valuable. It leads students to focus on collecting the information that is most relevant to their purposes rather than collecting quantities of random facts, and makes the whole task seem manageable. As always, the teacher is responsible for modeling and guiding students through this part of the process.

Students *gather information* from a variety of sources, such as informational books, magazines, newspapers, almanacs, atlases, and encyclopedias. In addition to these print sources, students should learn to use videotapes, films, and filmstrips, and to interview people who have expertise in the area they are studying. The teacher needs to demonstrate the process of recording information in the form of brief notes, rather than copying whole sentences or paragraphs. Elementary students are old enough to understand what plagiarism is and why it is wrong. Many teachers have found that the best way to prevent the habit of copying from developing in young children is to separate reading from notetaking. Children can spend time reading and taking in information and then (with the book closed and put away) record what they remember (Maxim, 1990; Collins, 1990). Notes in the form of key words or phrases may be recorded on note cards or cluster diagrams.

Older children can learn to set up and use data charts such as the one in Figure 4-3. The forms for data charts may be designed by hand or by a computer equipped with a simple data base program. Subtopics or questions they want answered are brainstormed and recorded along the top of the chart. Sources of information are listed down the side, and notes are recorded in the boxes.

To *organize the information for presentation*, students go over the information and make decisions about what to include and how to order and present their material in the most clear and interesting

THE ENDANGERED ELEPHANT				
Source of Information:	Evidence that elephants are an endangered species	Major causes	Uses of Ivory	What's being done to save elephants
Science text				
Natural History magazine date: ___				
Interview with M. Clark, environmental educator date ___				

Figure 4-3
Data Chart: The Endangered Elephant

way. They can be encouraged to create visual aids such as charts, pictures, or models, which tend to enhance audience understanding and enjoyment. Before delivering their report to an audience, speakers need to rehearse. This can be done outside of class or in class with a partner. Before presentations are given, it is a good idea to remind students of points they need to remember when speaking. Speakers should speak loudly enough for all to hear, look at their audience, stick to their key points using note cards, clusters, or data charts for reference, and remember to use their visual aids.

Students may *present their oral reports* to the whole class or to smaller groups of children. Kathy O'Dell had her third-graders give their reports on the human body to groups of five or six classmates at a time. Each afternoon she scheduled four speakers. They each went to a corner of the classroom and the other children, divided into listening groups, rotated around the room, listening to each report, asking questions or giving comments, and then moving on to the next speaker. Ms. O'Dell's rationale was twofold: children would give their first formal oral report to a small audience, which is less intimidating than a large one, and they would each get a chance to give their report four times. They practiced and refined their presentations because of the format she chose to use. Later in the year, when they were more experienced presenters, they gave reports in front of larger audiences, even videotaping one project. She also introduced ways in which she and the children in the audience could give speakers constructive feedback on the relevance of their content and the clarity and effectiveness of their presentations.

LOOKING BACK

In this chapter you have learned about some of the many ways that oral language can be used in elementary classrooms to enhance and extend students' learning and their enjoyment of the learning process. Students should learn to listen for different purposes and respond in appropriate ways. They should be involved in informal conversations, discussions, and more formal kinds of talk; all of these can be used extensively in connection with literature and literacy activities and also in the context of content area learning, which involves the exploration of information and ideas. Oral language weaves through the curriculum. Teachers can help children learn to use their oral language more skillfully and effectively by modeling and guiding their practice of the various processes involved in each of the different ways of using talk.

SELF-TEST

1. Name some factors that may affect the extent to which students attend while listening. What could you as a teacher do to help them attend better?

2. List the skills and competencies in oral language use that elementary language arts programs should develop.

3. Explain several ways in which oral language activities may enhance children's study of literature.

4. Explain the difference in purpose and form between discussions held before reading and after reading about a topic.

5. Demonstrate two strategies you could show students that would help them organize information in preparation for giving an oral report.

BIBLIOGRAPHY

Cambourne, B. (1990). *Read and retell.* Portsmouth, N.H.: Heinemann.

Cazden, C. (1986). Classroom discourse. In Whitrock, M.C. (ed.), *Handbook of research on teaching* (3rd ed.), New York: Macmillan, pp. 432-463.

Collins, P. (1990). Bridging the gap. In Atwell, N. (ed.), *Coming to know.* Portsmouth, N.H.: Heinemann.

DeStephano, J., Pepinsky, H. and Sanders, T. (1982). *Discourse rules and literacy learning in a classroom.* In Wilkinson, E. (ed.), *Communicating in the classroom.* New York: Academic Press.

Eeds, M. and Wells, D. (1989). Grand conversations: an exploration of meaning construction in literature study groups. *Research in the Teaching of English, 23,* 4-29.

Gambrell, C., Pfeiffer, W. and Wilson, R. (1985). The effect of retelling upon comprehension and recall of text information. *Journal of Educational Research, 78,* 216-220.

Hansen, J. (1987). *When writers read.* Portsmouth, N.H.: Heinemann.

Hennings, D. (1990) *Communication in action* (4th ed.). Boston: Houghton Mifflin.

Maxim, D. (1990). Beginning researchers. In Atwell, N. (ed.), *Coming to know.* Portsmouth, N.H.: Heinemann.

O'Donnell, M. and Wood, M. (1992). *Becoming a reader: a Developmental approach to reading instruction.* Boston: Allyn and Bacon.

Wendt, T. (1990). Units of study in an intermediate grade classroom. In Mills, H. and Clyde, J.A. (eds.), *Portraits of whole language classrooms.* Portsmouth, N.H.: Heinemann.

Wilen, W.W. (1986). *Questioning skills for teachers* (2nd ed.). Washington, D.C.: National Education Association.

Wolvin, A.D. and Coakley, C.G. (1979). *Listening instruction.* Urbana Ill.: National Council of Teachers of English.

5 Written Communication: Composing

Probably the teaching of writing has changed more in the past fifteen years than any other area of language arts instruction. Thanks largely to the pioneering work of Donald Graves, who studied and publicized the process young children go through when they are allowed and encouraged to take control of their own writing, elementary classrooms all across the United States now incorporate "writing workshops" based on the newer understandings of writing development and viable ways of facilitating children's growth as writers. In the best of today's elementary schools, children begin writing early, write frequently, and are members of a writing community. As one delighted parent remarked, with a tinge of amazement in her voice, "My daughter is only seven years old, and she considers herself an author!"

In this chapter we will look first at the writing of the youngest members of the elementary school community. Emergent writers are unique in their approaches to writing; consequently, the teaching, or facilitating, of writing in the kindergarten is different in many ways from the teaching of writing in later grades. Next we will focus on the writing process as it is used by most children in grades 1 through 6 (and beyond). Our examination of the writing process and the facilitation of writing development will include the steps writers go through in composing and finishing a piece of writing, the importance of sharing throughout the writing process, the teacher's changing roles in teaching writing, and the methods used to assess writing.

This chapter will focus on helping children to compose and on the content of their writing; teaching the conventions of writing will be addressed in chapter 6.

CAN YOU?

1. Demonstrate the five forms of writing that kindergartners commonly use?

2. Compare the "writing process approach" with old paradigm methods of teaching writing?

3. Explain the different ways children revise at different developmental stages?

4. Give a rationale for student control over selection of writing topics?

5. Explain the format and purpose of minilessons?

EMERGENT WRITING

In the past, it was generally assumed that children could not communicate through writing until they knew how to read and had mastered the conventional spellings of many words. The research and informed observation of young children over the past 20 years has changed our views. Today, children's early attempts at writing are recognized as an important element in their literacy development. Writing, in whatever form the child chooses, is encouraged and celebrated in early childhood classrooms, for we know that children learn to write in much the same way they learn to talk and to read—through experimentation. Emergent reading and writing are closely linked. As they see writing modeled and experiment with writing themselves, children construct and refine the knowledge about printed language that is necessary for learning to read and write conventionally.

On the basis of extensive observations, researcher Elizabeth Sulzby has described the forms of writing used spontaneously in kindergarten classrooms. She observed the following forms of writing:

- *Drawing* —When invited to write, the child draws. Many young children consider writing and drawing synonymous. When they write by drawing, they are using drawing to convey a message, and often "read" their drawings as though they were accompanied by print.

- *Scribble* —The child produces wavy lines or loops, often moving from left to right. Children who write in scribble seem to have a general notion of what writing looks like, and of the nature and purpose of writing.

- *Letter strings* —The child writes random strings of letters and letter-like marks. They sometimes include numbers. Children who have learned to write their names or some isolated letters and numbers reproduce these in random order to represent writing.

- *Invented spelling* —The child has become aware of letter-sound relationships and uses these in writing. At first whole words may be represented by single letters (*P* for "pumpkin," for example). As children develop more knowledge about letter-sound relationships, more speech sounds are represented in their spellings.

- *Conventional spelling* —Even kindergarten children who are a long way from reading conventionally will memorize the standard spellings of some words that are particularly meaningful to them. Conventionally spelled words may show up in the midst of writing that consists mostly of invented spelling (Sulzby, 1985; Sulzby, Barnhart, and Heishima, 1989; Wood, 1991).

Sulzby noted that these forms of writing do not constitute a clear developmental sequence. Emergent writers' selection of a form of writing is heavily influenced by the length and complexity of their message. For example, a kindergarten student might use invented spelling to write a one- or two-word caption for her picture, but switch to letter strings or scribble when composing a letter or story. In a study conducted by the author in which several children's writing was closely observed throughout their kindergarten year, some of the children used all five forms of writing toward the end of that year. Rather than replacing old forms with new ones, the children used new forms to add to their repertoire of choices of ways to write (Wood, 1991).

Like reading, writing develops in an environment where children see its functional use modeled by adults, where inviting materials and the time to use them are available, and where approximations are expected and accepted. Teachers need to respond to all children's writings, regardless of form, as meaningful messages. It is important to accept the different forms of writing used by kindergartners as equally valuable. Kindergarten teacher Laverne Knight bases her modeling of writing on Sulzby's recommendations. During the second week of school she draws her children together on the rug and explains to them that kindergartners have special ways of writing. She solicits children's input about what she might write, makes up a sentence, and then records it in each of the five forms (see Figure 5-1). She says, "I think I'll write, 'I wore my

Drawing:

Scribble:
(Loop-de-loop)   *eee onv hob leeheoo*

Letter Strings: M A V M L E

Invented Spelling: I WR M N RKT T SL.

Conventional: *I wore my new raincoat to school.*
(Grown up writing)

Figure 5-1 Kindergarten Forms of Writing

new raincoat to school.' If I were a kindergartner, I might write it this way." She picks up a felt-tip pen and draws a stick figure in a coat on the chart paper on the easel next to her. "Then," she says, "I might read it this way." Running her hand from left to right under the drawing, she says, "I wore my new raincoat to school."

"Or," she continues, "I might write it this way." She produces some loopy scribble. Sometimes a child asks if it is "cursive" writing. "Well, " she answers, "it looks sort of like cursive writing, doesn't it? But it's special kindergarten writing. I call it 'loop-de-loop!'" (Laverne has found that the word *scribble* has "babyish" connotations to many children, so she has renamed this form of writing.) "Then I might read it back this way." She runs her hand from left to right under the scribble as she says, "I wore my new raincoat to school." She continues in this way with the other forms of writing. As she produces the letter string, she mentions that she might just use the letters she knows how to write. For the invented spelling, she says the words slowly, mentioning the letter-sounds she hears and not spelling any of the words conventionally. She refers to the last form, conventional spelling, as "grown-up writing," and says, "Since I am a grown up, I would probably write it this way, in grown-up writing." She writes the sentence and reads it back conventionally.

Laverne does this sort of modeling every few weeks. She reports that it frees up her children, particularly those who are still unsure of the formation of many letters or who are not yet able to use letter-sound correspondences. Many children do not get the hang of invented spelling until well into first-grade. However, a teacher like Laverne Knight validates the legitimacy of their writing in forms that are developmentally appropriate for them. The children in her classroom never say, "I don't know how to write," for she has shown them that they do and that their work does not have to look like adult writing.

Beyond modeling, there are various ways to promote the exploration of writing in kindergarten classrooms. Some teachers create a writing center, a special area in the classroom where children can go to write whenever they have a choice of activities. The center includes a table and chairs, as well as a variety of accessible writing implements such as crayons, large and small pencils, felt-tip markers, and a chalkboard with chalk. Different sizes and types of paper are set out. Most of it should be unlined. Index cards and blank books (sheets of newsprint stapled together) are often included, as are inkpads and stamps, scissors, and tape. An alphabet chart should be within easy view, and there should be a bulletin board nearby on which children can display their writing.

Kindergarten children can engage in many writing projects that are functional and purposeful. They can make *greeting cards* for holidays and special occasions to be given to family members and friends. They can be encouraged to write *notes* to caregivers about what they are doing in school and *thank-you notes* to the parent who brings in cupcakes or the man who showed them around the farm on their field trip. They can help make *lists* of items they will need for a class party, or of things to write about in their journal, or of the people for whom they want to make Christmas or Hannukah cards. Some teachers designate an area on the bulletin board as a message board, where children can post *messages* they write to one another.

In addition to encouraging these types of writing activities, most teachers set aside a regular period of time every day for writing. During this time children often write in journals which the teacher prepares by stapling blank pieces of newsprint together in construction paper covers. Children are encouraged to write whatever they would like in their journals, choosing topics and forms of writing that best suit them. Kindergarten teachers sometimes worry that children's journals seem very repetitive. Classroom teacher Judith Hilliker collected the journal writings of several of her children to study this phenomenon. She found that the children's favorite topics for drawing, repeated over time, gradually became more embellished and were usually the basis for their first attempts to go beyond drawing and write a printed message. In her published classroom study, she reassures teachers that kindergartners' repetitions of favorite themes is not only normal, it seems to serve a valuable purpose for the young writers, as they develop "ownership" of a topic (Hilliker, 1988). When journal writing is incorporated as a regular part of the school day and continued throughout the year, children's entries usually show great gains in length, detail, and fluency (Newman, 1984).

Kindergarten children's growth as writers can be enhanced still further by the inclusion of some teacher-directed composing in the program. Children can be invited to react in various ways to literature that has been read aloud to them, or to write about a field trip, or to contribute to a collection of writings on a given topic, to be bound together and placed in the classroom library. The teacher-directed writings that Laverne Knight's students did during their kindergarten year included the following:

- A response to Joy Cowley's *The Big Toe,* showing to whom or what the toe actually belonged

- A "Mitten Story," written in a four-page booklet shaped like a mitten, after hearing Brett's *The Mitten* read aloud

Figure 5-2 Meagan: Kindergarten
"My big toe
My big toe
My big toe."

- "My Terrible, Horrible, No Good, Very Bad Day," written and bound into a class book after hearing Viorst's *Alexander and the Terrible, Horrible, No Good, Very Bad Day*

- Writing about what was seen on a field trip to an apple farm

- A five-page pop-up book of information about the sea and sea animals, which the class had been studying

Ms. Knight replaces journal writing time with a more teacher-directed composing activity every ten days or so. She always models the activity first for the children. For example, she made her own mitten story and created her own pop-up book, sharing with the

Figure 5-3 Jolene: Kindergarten
"You got my big toe."

children how she decided what to put on each page and how she drew and then wrote a message, as well as reading them her finished product. In these modeling sessions she often models forms of writing again or reminds children of the ways they could write.

If appropriate teacher modeling and direction are included in the curriculum, children are stretched to think about and attempt new genres or topics for writing that they probably would not otherwise try. Through such activities, teachers also have the opportunity to model sharing, an extremely important part of the writing process in kindergarten and at all grade levels. Whether children are writing on self-selected topics in their journals or on more teacher-directed topics, they should be given daily opportunities to share, to "read" their pieces to the teacher and their peers. Kindergartners learn to respond to the author by telling exactly what they liked in the piece and asking questions of the author about the piece or the process of authorship. Laverne Knight, like many teachers in higher elementary grades, has a special "author's chair" in her classroom. Each day at the end of writing time, the children gather in a circle on the rug, and the four children who are designated to share on that day take turns sitting in the author's chair, "reading" their writing to the group, and taking three or four questions from their peers. On the day when Alex shared his journal entry about Ninja Turtles, the following dialogue took place:

Ms. Knight: O.K., who has a question for Alex?

(Several children raise hands.)

Alex: Jonathan.

Jonathan: I like the way you drawed the Ninja Turtles. They look real, 'specially Donatello.

Alex: Anna.

Anna: How did... what made you decide to write about that?

Alex: Well I play Ninja Turtles a lot, and Donatello is my favorite one, so I like to write about him. ...Tim?

Tim: How did you learn to make their feet so good?

Alex: I draw them a lot. And my brother is good at drawing them and he showed me how to do it.

Ms. Knight: Thank you for sharing your story, Alex. We really enjoyed it.

The children in this class have taken their cues from their teacher's modeling of how to share a piece of writing, the kinds of questions that are genuine and supportive of the writer, and the way to manage a question-answer situation.

While assessment of writing will be addressed in a later section of this chapter, it is worth noting here that teachers of emergent writers need to be aware of other factors in addition to the forms of writing their children are using. Is the child able to sustain a topic over several pages (in topical booklets, for example)? Does the child pay attention to the print (in whatever form) when reading from the writing? Does the child "track" the print with a finger? Through children's writing the perceptive teacher can tell a great deal about the extent to which the child has developed basic concepts about printed language (see chapter 2). If the kindergarten provides an environment in which children are immersed in print and literacy experiences, and in which reading and writing are modeled repeatedly by a caring and enthusiastic teacher, children's understandings about the world of print will blossom and teachers will see evidence of this in their writing. A key point for kindergarten teachers to remember, however, is that young children spend a long time in approximating writing and that their particular writing behaviors and paths of development are astonishingly varied and unique. In other words, a wide range of writing behaviors are "normal" in kindergarten. Children should be immersed in print and in the modeling of its use; beyond this their individual paths and rates of development should be honored. In the words of Lesley Morrow, a well-known early childhood educator, "Children's early writings are to be enjoyed, valued, and understood. ...They should not be made the occasion for the hunting and correction of errors or for excessive direct teaching" (Morrow, 1989, p. 157).

THE WRITING PROCESS

Think back to your own elementary school experiences with writing. If they were typical, your teacher occasionally gave you a "creative" writing assignment, such as "A Day in the Life of a Sneaker." You were given 30 or 40 minutes to write your story; the teacher then collected the papers. You received your story back the next day with a grade (or perhaps two grades, one for "creativity," or content, and the other for correctness and neatness of form) and with errors marked in red. You may have been required to copy your composition over again, incorporating the teacher's corrections. Very likely the teacher was frustrated with most of the writing her students produced. You may have been one of the two or three students who wrote amusing, clever stories. However, several of your classmates produced only a sentence or two, and the majority of the other papers were mediocre. More likely than not they lacked description, were rather uninteresting, and were not coherent stories.

Teachers who use the traditional approach to writing often complain about the poor quality of the writing of most of their students and about the students' lack of motivation and outright dislike of writing. The problem is that these students have no ownership of their writing and no one is teaching them how to marshall their thoughts effectively and put them into written words. No one watches them write, shares techniques with them, or asks them about their composing strategies. The teacher is the sole audience for their writing. They are asked to perform difficult tasks that are, more often than not, unclear to them and that are unconnected with their own interests and concerns. Their teachers assign, evaluate, and correct writing. They do not truly teach writing.

There has been extensive research on writing and the teaching of writing in recent years. Because of what has been learned, the emphasis in writing instruction has shifted from product to process. The teacher who is current in his understanding of the research has expanded his roles to include facilitator of writing and member of the classroom writing community, working with his students to improve the processes as well as the products of writing. Figure 5-4 contrasts, in summarized form, the traditional and process approaches to teaching writing.

Much of the research that has fed into our understanding of the writing process has come from the reports and observations of accomplished writers about their own approaches to composing. We now know that successful writers, from first-graders to professional authors, follow a similar process of craft when they write. Teachers need to understand the components of this process in order to help

	The Traditional Approach	The Process Approach
Topic Selection	A specific creative writing assignment is made by the teacher.	Students choose their own topics, or topics are drawn from content-area study.
Instruction	Teacher provides little or no instruction. Students are expected to write as best they can.	Teachers teach students about the writing process and about writing forms.
Focus	The focus is on the finished product.	The focus is on the process that students use when they write.
Ownership	Students write for the teacher and feel little ownership of their writing.	Students assume ownership of their writing.
Audience	The teacher is the primary audience.	Students write for genuine audiences.
Collaboration	There is little or no collaboration.	Students write collaboratively and share writing in groups.
Drafts	Students write single-draft compositions in which they must focus on content and mechanics at the same time.	Students write rough drafts to pour out ideas and then revise and edit these drafts before making final copies.
Mechanical Errors	Students are required to produce error-free compositions.	Students correct as many errors as possible during editing but a greater emphasis is on content than on mechanics.
Teacher's Role	The teacher assigns the composition and grades it after completed.	The teacher teaches about writing and provides feedback during revising and editing.
Time	Students complete most compositions in less than an hour.	Students spend one, two, or three weeks working on a composition.
Assessment	The teacher assesses the quality of the composition after it is completed.	The teacher provides feedback while students are writing so they can use it to improve their writing. Assessment focuses on the process that writers use and the finished product.

Figure 5-4
Traditional and Process Approaches to Writing.
From Tompkins and Hoskisson (1991, p. 228), with permission.

each student find and use effective writing strategies. Theorists have named these components *prewriting, drafting, revising, editing,* and *publishing.*

Prewriting includes preparations for drafting a composition. Before beginning a draft, the writer selects a topic, identifies the intended audience for the writing and the purpose of the writing, and rehearses in some way. The preparation may include reading a book or collecting information from several sources. Young children often rehearse by drawing (Hilliker, 1988; Calkins, 1986). Older students are more likely to brainstorm or create notes, informal outlines, or webs (see chapter 4). Writers of all ages benefit greatly from oral rehearsal—talking about their topic with another writer who shows interest, asks them questions, and helps them define what they plan to say in their writing. Lucy Calkins (1986) describes rehearsal as "a way of living." People (including elementary school children) who anticipate that they are going to write frequently and regularly begin to be aware of potential topics all around them. They come to writing with a collection of possible topics to choose from and may find themselves mentally rehearsing for writing at many times other than the designated writing time.

Drafting is the preferred term for the next stage, rather than *writing,* because drafting implies a tentative product, a first try that is not intended or expected to be a polished product. The goal in drafting is to get the ideas down on paper. Some writers prefer to forge ahead without stopping until the draft is more or less complete, while others stop and start, rereading, pausing to think, and working over parts of the draft as they go. It is important, however, to teach children that all writers draft their pieces and go back later to make changes and attend to surface correctness. If an unskilled writer is constantly worrying about errors and searching for correct spellings or is starting over every time time a smudge or line-out appears on the paper, fluency is destroyed. We must free children to concentrate on the content of their writing during drafting, with the assurance that they will have plenty of opportunity to make changes and to "clean it up" later.

Revision means, literally, "seeing again." Young or very unskilled writers, for whom getting even a few words down on paper is a struggle, do not revise, or they revise orally, as illustrated by this conversation between a first-grade teacher and one of her students:

Teacher: This is a fine picture of you and your dog, Mindy. And could you read me what you wrote?

Mindy: (tracking her invented spelling with her finger) My new puppy plays with me.

Teacher: What kind of things does he do when you play together?

Mindy: He has this old sock, and I hold it and he bites it real hard and shakes his head.

Teacher: Does he act fierce?

Mindy: (laughing) Yes. And he even growls.

Teacher: That tells us a lot more about him. Do you think you could add some of that to your writing?

Mindy: No. No. It's finished.

As writers become more fluent, they are better able to add, subtract, or rearrange information to make their writing more closely match their intent. Revision is often stimulated by sharing the draft in conferences with individuals or groups that ask the writer questions, thus helping him view the writing from the audience perspective. More mature, experienced writers develop the ability to ask themselves questions, as it were, to stand back from their writing, read it, and work at saying what they want to say more clearly or effectively.

Editing is the final step in preparing a final draft and involves attention to surface features such as spelling and punctuation. Thorough editing is only necessary if a piece is to be published or displayed to an audience. Children should take increased responsibility for proofreading and editing as they gain fluency and maturity. In the beginning (first grade) the teacher or another skilled writer (a parent aide or older child) does most of the editing for or with the child when a piece is being prepared for publication. Children are taught to proofread, using editing checklists or working with peers, as they become capable of doing so. Mastering the conventions of writing comes much more easily to some children than it does to others. (Poll your class and you will find that even well-educated adults vary considerably in their ability to proofread and to spell correctly.) Teachers must help writers to steadily improve their ability to edit independently without overwhelming them; when they have gone as far as they can reasonably be expected to go in editing a piece of writing, we finish the job for them, if the piece is to be published. This is the same procedure followed by professional, published writers.

In one second-grade classroom I visited, the teacher had summarized the writing process in a way that could be understood and used by second-graders. In the beginning of the year, as he worked through the writing process with the children, they became familiar with the terminology of writing process and experienced each of its components. A poster hung on the wall as a reminder to the children and to help inform visitors to the classroom of the approach being used.

Our Writing Process

Prewriting: We choose a topic. We read, look, listen, talk, draw.

Drafting: We write about our topic. Now is the time to put down as many ideas as we can. (We'll check spelling, punctuation, and penmanship *later*.)

Revising: We read our writing to our teacher or our friend or our class. They ask questions about what we have written. Then we may want to add information or take something out.

Editing: Now we check our spelling and punctuation. We correct the things we know. Then we get help from a friend or from the teacher.

Publishing means "going public" with a piece of writing, sharing it with an audience. Knowing that a piece is going to be published in some form motivates writers to revise, to edit, to make the work their very best. Children's work can be published in the form of homemade hardcover books (see appendix B), stapled, construction-paper-covered booklets, magazines, class anthologies, local or school newspapers, bulletin board displays, or in the plastic-covered pages of photograph albums. For children, as for all writers, publishing should be the final step in the writing process, and works for publication should be selectively chosen. It is neither realistic nor desirable for children to publish everything they write. Only what they consider their best work is generally brought to publication. Many teachers require children to complete several pieces before choosing one to publish.

All children should publish because publishing and seeing others read their work makes them feel like insiders, like authors, and because it concretizes the close relationship between writing and reading. As Donald Graves (1983) reminds us, publishing should not be "the privilege of the classroom elite, the future literary scholars. Rather, it is an important mode of literary enfranchisement for each child in the classroom" (p. 55).

Although it is important for teachers to be conversant with the parts of the writing process described here, it is equally important for them to realize that writing is not produced in a neat, sequential series of steps. Actually the writing process is recursive. A writer may rehearse and plan for 30 seconds or many days; once she begins drafting she may go back to prewriting (to get more information or revise her outline), draft some more, reread and revise her beginning, cross out and replace a word, continue with drafting, and so on. Another writer may make no changes or revisions until his first draft is completed. We all have our preferred ways of approaching writing. Moreover, our approaches differ according to the type of writing we are attempting. We must remember that, except for publishing, the components of the writing process are just that—components—not really "steps" as they are often called. What most writers do is focus or concentrate on one component after another as the writing progresses.

There are two additional important ingredients of the writing process as it occurs in the context of classrooms. These are modeling and sharing. The teacher must model, repeatedly, every part of the writing process, from topic selection to publishing. Students must see their teacher as a writer—an experienced writer who shares strategies and techniques with them, but who also struggles with his or her own writing. Sharing is also important at every point along the way in writing, not just when a piece is completed. Students need to discuss their topics before drafting, get input from others during the drafting process, try out their drafts on others to see what revisions might be called for, and help each other with editing. Finally, they need to share and celebrate their finished, published pieces.

DEVELOPMENTAL EXPECTATIONS AND WRITING PROCESS

From first grade on, children engage in the writing process as previously described. However, the level at which they engage in each phase of the process differs according to their maturity and experience as writers. Teachers' expectations should be based on their knowledge of what is developmentally appropriate for their students. As you read the following description of behaviors, bear in mind that grade levels mentioned are approximate and that an individual child's status on the continuum of literacy development will be a more important determinant of his writing behaviors than will his grade placement.

Beginning writers (almost all first-graders and many second-graders) make extensive use of drawing as a prewriting activity. In fact, they often select their topic on the basis of what they decide to draw (Calkins, 1986). Because print is still such an unfamiliar medium for them, their drawings carry much of the message of their composition. Their printed messages generally start with simple labels for parts of their drawings and gradually extend into phrases and sentences (Karelitz, 1988). Their drafts are short and are usually completed in one session. Revision in response to questions or comments generally consists of oral additions or details added to the drawing. Editing is done primarily by the teacher. Publishing can be accomplished frequently because pieces are short. Two or three publications per month for each child is a reasonable goal (Graves, 1983). The published texts are generally produced by an adult and illustrated by the child.

As children gain fluency in writing (generally in second and third grade), their drawing ceases to drive their writing, and illustrations become supplementary to written text, produced after the text is complete. Brainstorming, reading, and webbing become appropriate prewriting activities. Drafts are longer, often taking several days to complete. Revisions are more likely to be undertaken if the writer has a conference with peers or the teacher before the draft is finished. Frequent (daily) conferences and sharing of writing in pairs or in small or large groups is ideal. By the time they are in third grade, most children revise by making additions (at any point in their text) or by writing alternative beginnings and endings. They can now proofread and edit with peers or alone, using simple editing check-

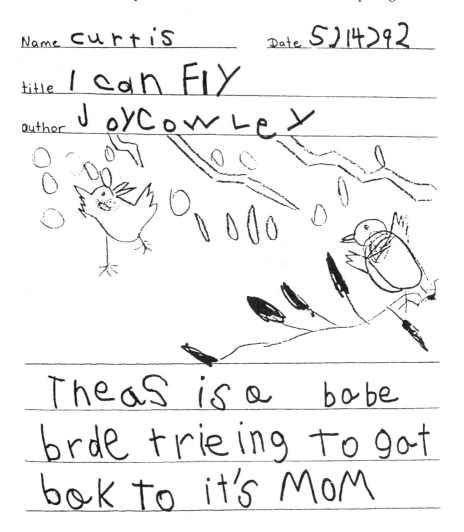

Name curtis   Date 5)14)92

title I can FIY

author J oYCowLeY

Theas is a babe
brde trieing to got
bok to it's MoM

Figure 5-5
First-Grader's Writing Sample

lists and lists of words they are responsible for spelling convention-ally. The secret to success with starting children on the road to eventual competence as editors is to limit expectations and to focus on a selected and manageable (from the child's point of view) number of items for which the writer is responsible. Final editing for publication is done by the teacher. Children publish less frequently as their pieces become longer. Publications are still usually produced by adults or under their direction and supervision.

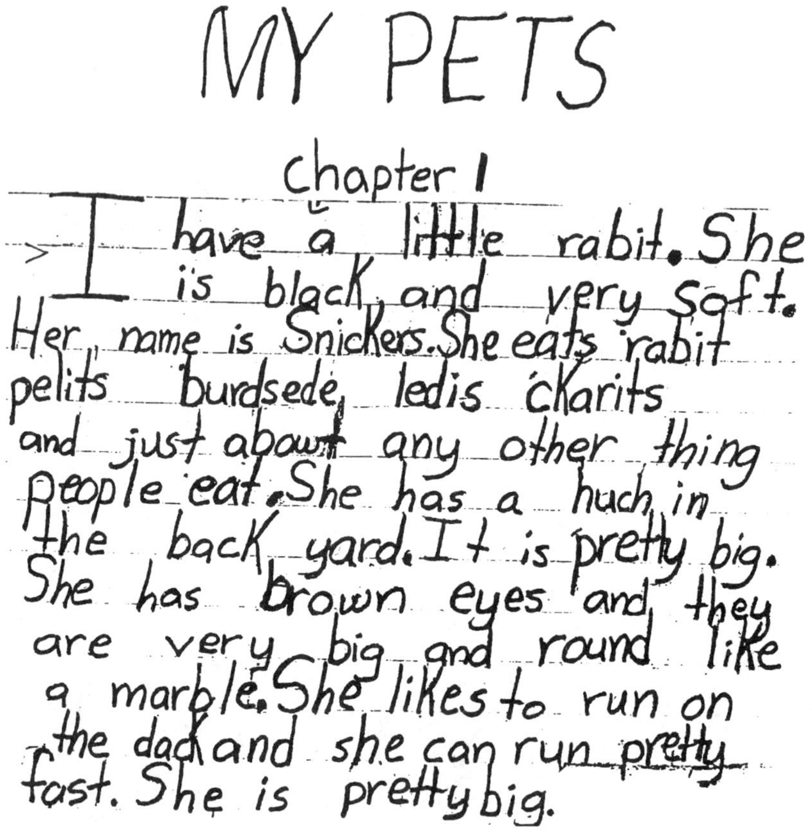

MY PETS

Chapter 1

I have a little rabit. She is black and very soft. Her name is Snickers. She eats rabit pelits burdsede, ledis charits and just about any other thing people eat. She has a huch in the back yard. It is pretty big. She has brown eyes and they are very big and round like a marble. She likes to run on the dad and she can run pretty fast. She is pretty big.

Figure 5-6
Third-Grader's Writing Sample (First Draft)

Most children who have had extensive opportunities to write in the primary grades are quite fluent by the time they reach fourth grade. In the upper elementary grades a variety of prewriting strategies may be modeled and used by children, including reading, discussion, webbing, and simple outlining. Their drafts are longer, and they may sustain interest in a piece over a number of days. They need to confer less frequently and benefit from substantial blocks of uninterrupted writing time. Their peer conferences become longer and more guided by the writer, who asks the audience for specific feedback. Many third- and fourth-graders go through a phase of producing long, unnecessarily detailed, and often redundant narratives. (These are often referred to as "bed-to-bed" narratives.) These students can be helped to learn to make subtractive revisions (deletions). Writers at this stage also become capable of revising by re-writing portions of the piece or even creating a whole new version, and by rearranging the order of parts of the piece. Students in the upper elementary grades can gradually assume more responsibility

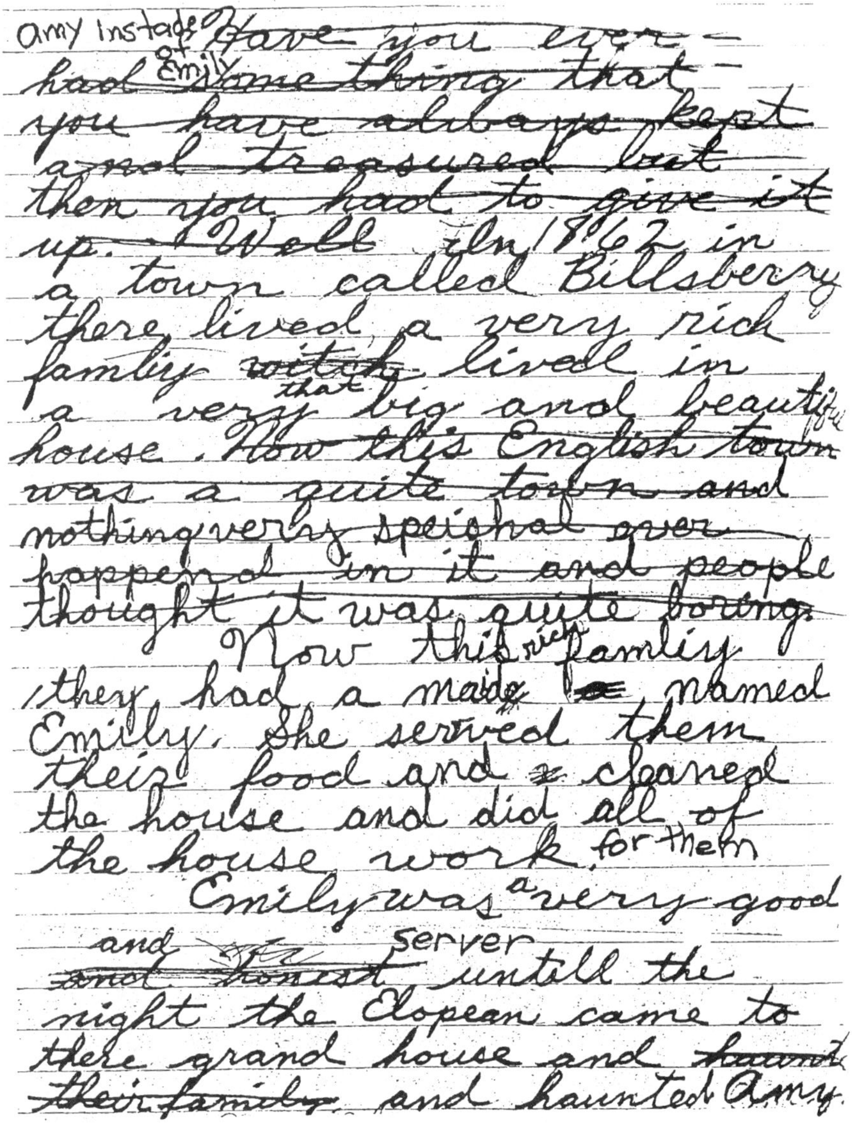

Amy Instead of Emily Have you ever had something that you have always kept and treasured but then you had to give it up. Well In 1962 in a town called Billsberry there lived a very rich family with that lived in a very big and beauti[ful] house. How this English town was a quite town and nothing very speical ever happened in it and people thought it was quite boring. Now this rich famliy they had a maid be named Emily. She served them their food and cleaned the house and did all of the house work for them. Emily was a very good and honist server untill the night the Clopean came to there grand house and haunt their family and haunted Amy.

Figure 5-7
Fifth-Grader's Writing Sample
First Draft (partial)

The Elopen
by
Leah Nista

In 1862 in a town called Billsberry there lived a very rich family that lived in a very big and beautiful house.

Now this rich family, they had a maid named Amy. She served them their food and she did all of the house-work for them.

Amy was a very good server until the night the Elopen came to to their grand house and haunted Amy.

An Elopen is an English spirit that is a real nusance to people.

Figure 5-8
Fifth-Grader's Writing Sample
Final Draft (partial)

for editing as they gain control over the conventions of print. Teachers still help to prepare pieces that will be published, however. Typically, students at this level publish perhaps four or five times a year, and they produce publications more independently than previously, typing or carefully writing text, making book covers, if those are used, and binding them independently.

SOME OBSERVATIONS ON TOPIC SELECTION

In the old paradigm of language arts instruction, the teacher assigned topics for students to write about most or all of the time and then spent considerable energy "motivating" the students to write. Students rarely felt inspired or truly invested in writing because (in part, at least) the topics did not usually reflect issues of central importance to them. Writers of all ages produce the best writing and invest the most in the writing process when they are dealing with topics that they know about and care about. When children are given guidance on how to select topics they know and care about, they are far more likely to commit themselves to the hard work of writing, and to feel real ownership of what they produce (Graves, 1983). Topic selection affects every other aspect of the writing process; it deserves considerable attention. Perhaps at some time in your own schooling you were told, "Today, children, we are going to do creative writing. You may write about anything you like. You may write a poem, or a story, or anything you feel like. I expect you to use your imaginations."

After a steady diet of teacher-assigned writing, you may have found it very difficult to come up with a topic. Limitless choices often result in the feeling that there is nothing worth writing about; in such situations some children beg the teacher to assign them a topic. While it is true that the best, most appropriate topics usually come from the writer, children need guidance in generating viable topics. As in other aspects of writing, teacher modeling sets the stage. Teachers can talk with students about the kinds of things that make good topics and about the need to spend some time thinking about one's life and interests in terms of possible writing topics. Cheryl Preston, a fourth-grade teacher, models topic selection by thinking of three topics of her own that fourth-graders might relate to. One day during the first week of school, in writing workshop time, she jots down three titles on the board:

The Sledding Accident

The Private Tree House

Putting Out the Garbage

She tells the children that it helps to have some choices about what to write about—but not too many. Three is a good number. She reads her titles with them and says, "I am not sure which one I want to write about. If I tell about them, it will help me decide." She then proceeds to tell a little bit about each topic: about the time when she was in fourth grade and her sled went out of control on icy snow, flew across a stream, and crashed into the opposite bank, giving her a bloody nose; about the tree house that she and her best friend built when they were nine, where they kept a tin box of treasures and escaped from their brothers and sisters; and about the arguments in her family over who is responsible for putting out the garbage, and why it is the chore everyone tries to avoid. The fourth-graders give rapt attention, ask her questions, and tell her which topic they hope she will write about. She then asks them to take a couple of minutes to think (without talking) and jot down three ideas of things they could write about. Because the topics Ms. Preston shares come from her personal experience, the students are likely to come up with topics of their own that would lend themselves to personal narratives. It is noteworthy, too, that one of the topics (Putting Out the Garbage) is very everyday; it is not based on an exciting or unusual event. This helps the teacher convey to the students that even seemingly mundane things can make very good topics. Children are less likely to say, "I don't have anything to write about; nothing ever happens to me."

Rehearsal before writing is tremendously helpful. When her students have each jotted down two or three possible topics, Ms. Preston has them pair up and talk briefly about each topic with their partners. At the end of five or six minutes, most of them are ready and eager to begin writing. Teachers and education students who go through this same exercise in the generation and sharing of three topics report several consistent outcomes of the sharing. Many people find that talking about their topic helps them to narrow its focus or to remember details they had not thought of originally. They also frequently report that listening to someone else's topics triggers new ideas for possible topics of their own. I often hear remarks such as, "That reminded me of something almost the same that happened to me."

As the school year progresses, Ms. Preston introduces other fruitful strategies for generating topics, including the following:

- Pairing up and interviewing partners about themselves, their families, and their hobbies and interests. After each interview the interviewer suggests areas covered that he or she thinks would be topics of interest to others.

- Gathering in a circle and sharing family legends (stories about family members or incidents that have been passed down from one generation to the next), objects of sentimental value, memories of security toys or blankets, impressions of what it means to be a brother or sister, or any other common experiences that touch on students' lives and feelings. Since reading Lucy Calkins' book, *Living Between the Lines* (1991), which documents the value of such sharing, Ms. Preston has had her students come together about once every two weeks for structured conversations of this type. After each discussion, the children add to their lists of possible topics.

- Having each student staple a page entitled "Topics" on the inside cover of the writing folder in which all of his or her writing is kept. Students are reminded to jot down possible topics whenever they occur to them.

- Brainstorming together about areas of expertise or special interest. Early in the year, Ms. Preston asks all students to name one topic on which they consider themselves an expert. She writes their contributions (which cover a wide range, from roller blading to eating ice cream to poisonous snakes) on the board. Once again, others' topics often remind students of possibilities for themselves.

But what about teacher-assigned topics, you may be wondering? Is there a valid place for them in the curriculum? Although experts are not in full agreement on the answer to this question, most see teacher-directed writing as a legitimate and desirable component of a writing curriculum. The issues that arise have to do with the proportion of student-selected to teacher-selected topics. Some of the advantages of teacher-directed writing are that it broadens children's writing experiences, leading them to try topics or genres they might not select on their own, and that it provides students with a somewhat common writing experience to draw on for whole-class discussion and instruction. The potential disadvantage is loss of the motivation, control, and involvement that children are most likely to exhibit when they are writing about topics that are chosen by them because of personal relevance. Balance is essential. Many teachers direct children's writing when it is based on content-area study, but allow (or require) them to select their own topics for the everyday writing workshop. We must remember, too, that choice can and often should be allowed within a teacher's assignment. For example, all sixth-graders may be required to gather research and write a report on life in medieval times, but they can pick an area to focus on within this broad topic (Collins, 1990). When a teacher is engaging students in the reading and writing of poetry, biography, or fantasy, she may ask them to try writing in this genre, but leave the topic of their piece up to them. It is important to note that regardless of whether the topic is selected with or without teacher input, the components of the writing process should be honored.

THE WRITING CONFERENCE

Because sharing is such an important part of the writing process, writing conferences play a prominent role in effective writing instruction. Conferences may take place at any point in the process and may be between students or between student and teacher. Many teachers check in with each student periodically, but leave the bulk of the sharing to peers until a draft is finished or revised, at which point they meet with the student for final revision and editing. Other teachers set up a regular schedule, meeting with each student (either individually or in a small group) once a week, on their assigned day, to work with whatever the student seems to need at that point and to monitor the week's progress. Ways of managing conferences and fitting them into writing workshop vary; the important thing is to ensure that conferences take place, and take place frequently.

Conferences help writers by giving them an audience, providing support, and helping them to see their writing from a reader's perspective. Conferences help teachers to keep in close touch with their students, to learn about each child's path of development as a writer (and thereby to help appropriately), and to capitalize on "teachable moments," those moments when a child has a clear need for a strategy or for information and is therefore extremely receptive to learning it. Susan Sowers (1988) reminds us, "a good conference is a workmanlike conversation about writing in progress—not an interrogation" (p. 130). Neither is it a critique. The purpose of every conference is ultimately to support the writer.

Elementary students are capable of providing valuable feedback to each other through *peer conferences.* Young writers need more sharing and feedback than one teacher can possibly provide. Moreover, students value their peers' opinions and ideas and are actually more likely to rework their writing if they have had input from their peers. For these reasons it clearly makes sense to teach children to work with each other on their writing. Teachers who have not had experiences with peer conferences often fear that the children will criticize each others' work and use negative or even cruel comments. This does not happen, however, if the teacher shows students how to hold constructive conferences and sets some guidelines for them to follow. Once again, teacher modeling is crucial. Students will imitate the type and the tone of the teacher's comments to them.

A good way to introduce children to constructive conferring is to read aloud a piece you have written and ask them to do two things: first, tell you something specific that they liked about your piece, and then ask you any questions they have about the subject. When they have done this, you can explain to them that specific comments help you to know what you have done well as a writer. This will help you in future writing. (Examples of appropriate comments are, "I liked your beginning. I was interested right away." Or, "I liked the description of your grandmother's old fashioned boots. I could really picture them." A comment such as "I liked your story," is not specific enough to be useful.) You may also tell them that their questions led you to see some things you might want to change or add to your piece as you work on it some more. Then ask students to use the same format when they confer with a partner. The writer reads his or her piece aloud to the listener. The listener responds by telling something specific that he or she liked about the piece, and then asks questions about (or discusses) the content of the piece.

As students become more experienced with conferences, they will spontaneously move beyond this simple format. Writers must learn to ask their partners for the kind of feedback they want. "I've written two beginnings and I'm not sure which one I like best. I want you to tell me what you think," says fifth-grader James to his partner. " I added the things we talked about yesterday," says sixth-grader Shyla. "I want you to listen to it again and tell me if anything is still confusing." Second-grader Marcy hands her piece to her friend Cammie. "I'm almost ready to publish my story," she says. "I've checked it over, but I want you to see if I spelled anything else wrong and if I put in all the periods right." There are many purposes for peer conferences. As a rule, children should read their writing aloud to their partners (keeping the focus on content), unless they are engaged in editing.

Teacher-student conferences become more and more genuinely helpful to both teacher and student as the teacher gains experience conferring with children. As teachers, we feel a responsibility to nudge children along, to speed up their learning, and, when it comes to writing, to see the results of our teaching in their products. We must constantly remind ourselves that the goal of a conference is not to get the child to revise the piece in such a way that it is more satisfying to us. It is easy to be too directive ("I think you need to add more details") or to manipulate the child's revisions indirectly through clever questions and comments ("Don't you think it would be more interesting for your reader if you added more details about how your aunt looked?"). Many children are willing to make suggested changes to please the teacher. While they may end up with a piece of writing that is "better" in our eyes, they will have lost some ownership of the writing and may well not have learned any strategies they could use independently in the future. Lucy Calkins (1986) reminds us that teachers should teach the writer, not the writing. Our role in conferences is to support, to learn, to facilitate insights, and to gradually build the ability to convey meaning clearly and effectively in writing.

Teachers sometimes ask for (or generate) lists of questions to use in conferences with students. We should be cautious in using such lists, because each conference is a unique interaction, with questions or comments flowing from responses and situations, not from a pre-determined list. There really are no magic questions. Teachers need to focus on listening, on hearing the student. Donald Graves (1983) stresses the importance of letting the child lead in conferences. The discussion often begins with "How's it going?" or "What are you working on today?" and ends with "What are you going to do next?" Although there are no set questions to use in between, a help-ful pattern to follow when you feel you need one is the following:

- Find out how things are going for the writer.

- "Reflect" the child's writing back to her by paraphrasing or sum-marizing what she has written. (Some teachers teach children to do this in peer conferences, and call the process "say back.")

- "Expand" by talking or getting the student to talk about the sub-ject. Is there anything she wishes to add? If so, where?

- Is any part of the draft especially pleasing or troublesome to the writer?

- Where does she plan to go next with the piece?

Susan Sowers (1988) summarizes important implications for in-struction through conferences. Helpful points include the following:

1. Don't expect to find a cause-effect or stimulus-response relation-ship between a question and a student's revision....Regular sup-port—time for writing, thoughtful discussion in conference, au-dience response from readings and publication, and explicit cri-teria for good writing—is more important than the right ques-tion. The results are long-term and cumulative.

2. Ask questions you want students to ask themselves....What they can do with you today they will do on their own later.

3. Ask the writer questions you do not know the answers to. No one knows exactly how the writer will finish the piece. The con-ference is a kind of collaboration, a form of working together more common at home, at work, and at play than at school.

4. Ask students what questions or comments helped them to revise. Ask students what questions they ask themselves and what advice they give themselves (pp. 140, 141).

THE TEACHER'S CHANGING ROLES

Teachers have traditionally served primarily as assigners and evaluators of writing. In writing-process classrooms they must take on more varied roles. A writing teacher serves, at different times, as instructor, coach, facilitator/manager, and evaluator. When the process approach to writing first became popular, many teachers more or less abdicated the role of *instructor* because they were trying to free their curricula from the excessive teacher direction of the past. They found, however, that a writing program that was completely student centered often resulted in the production of large amounts of student writing over the course of a year without much evidence of improvement. Language arts educators are now aware of the need for a balance of teacher and student direction of the writing program. Calkins (1986) identifies as most effective those classrooms that have both high teacher input and high student input within the writing program.

One technique that provides opportunities for direct, whole-group teaching is the "minilesson" (Calkins, 1986; Atwell, 1987), which most often begins the writing workshop. Minilessons focus on some aspect of the writing process or the craft of writing that the teacher feels needs attention. Sometimes the minilessons have to do with managing the writing workshop (expectations about the students' use of writing folders, for example). At other times they focus on aspects of topic selection, revision, editing, conducting peer conferences, and publishing. The content of the minilessons should arise out of the teacher's observations of the children's work and her sense of what they need to enhance their skill as writers or to make the writing workshop run more smoothly and productively. In other words, the best minilessons do not come from a textbook or even from a brainstormed list of grade-level concerns; they evolve from the children's work and the teacher's goals for them. Whenever possible, minilessons should also help children to use the literature they have read or listened to for ideas and models. Minilessons can help students make connections between reading and writing.

Calkins stresses that minilessons should be direct, simple, and brief (less than ten minutes, as a rule). The teacher explains, demonstrates, or directs, rather than questions or elicits discussions. (These modes of instruction are used at other points in the writing process.) The expectation should be that some children will use the information from the minilesson immediately, but others will store it away to use later, perhaps needing a reminder. As an example, here is a minilesson which third-grade teacher John Polermo conducted with his students when he noticed the titles of many of their pieces were obvious and unimaginative:

Mr. Polermo had written a brief piece about his daughter bringing home a stray kitten. He copied his piece onto an overhead transparency so he could share it with the class. At the beginning of the piece he had written the title, *The Kitten*. He read the piece aloud as his third-graders followed along. Then he said, "I'm not happy with the title. It seems uninteresting, and I don't think it really tells what the piece is about. I looked at titles of animal stories to see what other authors had come up with. Lots of times they use the name of the animal; remember when we read *Old Yeller*? But sometimes the titles are really unusual, like *Where the Red Fern Grows,* or specific, like *Clifford's Halloween.* When I read my piece over a couple of times, I decided it was really about how my daughter Sarah convinced us to keep the kitten. I thought up a couple more titles, which I'll write over here on the side of the page, so I won't forget them." (He wrote, *Homeless No More* and underneath that, *Sarah Saves a Kitten*.) "I'll just leave them there and later I'll come back to this and make a decision about which one to use. Or maybe I'll think of another one. In your writing, you may want to check the titles of your pieces, especially of the one you're working on now. See if they're interesting, and if they really reflect what your piece is about. Jot down some choices, and you can discuss them in your conference if you want to. O.K., let's get on with our writing."

Mr. Polermo resisted the temptation to ask all students to take out their pieces and spend 15 minutes discussing and revising titles immediately after the minilesson. This would have been inappropriate for students who either were satisfied with the titles they had or were in the middle of drafting, and attention to the title would have taken valuable time away from writing. Several children did revise titles, however, and others discussed titles when they met for conferences with each other or Mr. Polermo. Their awareness had been raised, so the lesson was successful.

A great deal of the teacher's participation in writing workshop is in the roles of *coach* and *facilitator/manager.* By giving the writing workshop a predictable structure and making expectations clear to the students, the teacher sets the tone for serious work and productivity within a supportive framework. This takes good organization and planning on the part of the teacher, because children will very likely be at different points in the writing process at any given time, working on their own topics at their own rate. To keep track of all this, many teachers begin the writing workshop with a check on the status of the class. They take a few minutes to read each child's name and record what the child plans to work on that day. The children report the name of their piece or the topic and indicate whether they need a conference with another student or with the teacher, or whether they are ready to publish. Teachers devise abbreviations for recording this information. From the daily record of the status of the class, the teacher can tell something about the progress each child is making with his or her work. Figure 5-9 shows part of a status-of-the-class chart from Mr. Polermo's third-grade class.

As the workshop progresses, Mr. Polermo often marks the notes in the chart to indicate that the student did what was planned (had a conference, shared with the class, etc.). He sometimes jots a brief note such as "seems stuck" or "edited w. Jason."

A major consideration in managing writing instruction is the structuring of time. It is generally recommended that students have a regular writing time that they can count on every day, if possible. Donald Graves states that "at least four forty-five to fifty minute periods [per week] are necessary to provide a strong writing experience. The teacher starts with four thirty-five-minute periods and then expands, as both teacher and children learn to use the time well." (Graves, 1983, p. 90.) When teachers ask how they can devote this amount of class time to writing, he advises them to make the time by taking it, if necessary, from handwriting, spelling, and language study, or even from reading, pointing out that writing pro-

	Mon. 1/6	Tue. 1/7	Wed. 1/8	Th. 1/9	Fri. 1/10
Billy	Snake Story D	Snake Story D	S.S. c	S.S. T, Sh	S.S. * Lucky Penny D
Tonya	abs	The Dream c	The Dream T	Stray Cat D	Stray Cat D
Mendalio	Brothers T, *	Garbage Weekend D	Garbage Weekend c, D	G.W. D, c	G.W. D, Sh
Michelle	Christy c, D	Christy D	Christy D, T	Police Horse c, D	P. Horse D
Angela	Set of poems D	Set poems c, D	Set poems, Neighbors D (T)	Poems →	Set poems * Neighbors D
Carlos	skateboarding D	sk. D	sk c	sk D, T	abs

D=draft
C= conference
T= teacher
Sh = whole class share
* = ready to publish

Figure 5-9 Status of the Class (partial)

duces gains in all those curricular areas, *if* sufficient time and skillful help are provided. In the upper grades when children have begun to feel competent and experienced as writers, they will do more writing on their own and in the context of other subject areas. Less time will then be needed for a discrete writing time. Figure 5-10 shows the writing-workshop structures of two teachers.

Teachers facilitate writing by providing predictable, structured environments for student writers. Teachers must have high expectations and at the same time offer support and encouragement. They serve as guides to their students. Through example, they promote a business-like but accepting atmosphere where risks may safely be taken and each student's ideas, interests, and efforts are valued.

In a classroom where a process approach to writing instruction is used, assessment of children's progress is ongoing; while the teacher serves as the lead *evaluator,* the students play a role in evaluation as well. Progress in writing is best documented by keeping samples of students' work which may be compared to show growth over time.

<u>Mr. Polermo, grade 3</u>

5-8 min.   Minilesson

5 min.   Status of the class check

10 min.   S.S.W. (sustained silent writing) time
            No interactions. Everyone, including teacher, is thinking,
            planning, drafting, revising, or rereading and editing.

20 min.   Workshop time
            Some keep writing, others hold conferences or work
            together on revising or editing. Teacher meets with
            students who need his help or who he needs to monitor.
            He meets with each student about twice a week.

<u>10 min.</u> Whole class share
50 min.

<u>Ms. Feldman, grade 5</u>

5-8 min.   Minilesson

5 min.   Status of the class check

25 min.   Workshop time
            Writing: teacher goes from student to student for brief
            conferences. Up to four pairs of students may confer at
            designated conference areas in room.
            _____
35 min.

This schedule is followed on Monday, Wednesday, and Thursday. On
Tuesday Ms. Feldman meets for longer conferences (often in small groups)
with students who are stuck or who have completed revised drafts, and on
Friday she has a shorter writing period (20 minutes) which she usually
devotes to whole class sharing and discussion of students' writing.

Figure 5-10
Sample Schedules for Writing Workshop

Most teachers have their children keep all writing in a special writing folder rather than take it home. There are several advantages to this. First, it demonstrates to the children that their written products are considered valuable enough to store in a special place and save. Second, this system allows children to look back over their previous writings at any time. They may return to a discarded piece, go to previous writings for ideas, or take note of the types of writing they have done and the topics they have chosen. They date their drafts and staple them together if they do more than one, so that the evolution of each piece of writing is evident. Last and perhaps most important, the writing folder greatly facilitates evaluation of progress in all aspects of writing, including willingness to try new topics and genres, length and extent of development of ideas, language use, sentence sense, spelling and mechanics. The use of writing folders enables teacher and student or teacher and parent to examine primary evidence of the evolution of the student's skill as a writer.

Many teachers devise simple checklists to help them summarize and organize information gleaned from the writing folders. Sample assessment forms for the different stages of literacy development may be found in appendix C.

Assigning grades for writing is something that "goes against the grain" for most teachers. How can one possibly reduce a person's ideas, effort, and skill to a judgment in the form of a letter? And yet grading is a fact of life in most school systems—if not in the primary grades, then later on. In grading language arts work, teachers must generally make the best of a less than perfect situation. There are guidelines teachers can follow to reduce the potentially damaging effect of grades on children's opinions of themselves as writers and to make grading as fair as possible. First of all, students should not be graded (in "writing") on any work that they have not had the opportunity to revise and edit to the best of their ability. In fact, many experts maintain that we should not grade individual pieces of writing at all. Graves (1983) suggests that children be allowed to choose what they consider to be their (four or five) best pieces of work for the term and submit those, collectively, as the basis for a grade. Atwell (1988) describes evaluation conferences, held with each child toward the end of the grading period. Teacher and student go over selected pieces of writing together, assess progress toward the individual goals set at at the beginning of the quarter, and set new goals for the next quarter. The grades of Atwell's eighth-graders reflect her "sense of each student's growth in many areas—topic selection, level of involvement, clarity and grace of language, degree of effort and initiative, completeness of content, and consistency of editing and proofreading" (p. 237). Grades are ultimately assigned by the teacher, but only after significant input from and self-evaluation by each student. By sharing the criteria and method of grading with students, by evaluating them on the basis of their best work, and by soliciting their participation in the evaluation process, the grading process will remain as constructive as possible.

LOOKING BACK

Our treatment of written communication began with a discussion of the emergent writing that is most commonly seen in kindergarten children. The forms of writing that they use reflect their growing understanding of the purpose, nature, and function of printed language. The knowledgeable teacher encourages them to write daily, accepting the forms of writing they use as developmentally appropriate approximations.

As students move toward more conventional use of print, teachers can guide them through the components of the writing process: prewriting or rehearsal, drafting, revising, editing, and sometimes publishing. We have seen that teacher modeling and sharing through group work or conferences are essential to children's growth as writers. Teachers' roles have expanded beyond those of assigner and evaluator of writing to include facilitator, collaborator, instructor, and supportive guide. To teach writing effectively, the teacher must become an expert at structuring and orchestrating the various components of the writing workshop in such a way that children have uninterrupted time to write and receive the support, feedback, and "nudging" they need. Composing is complex; it requires the integration of many processes and competencies. Growth is gradual and cumulative and may best be documented through collected samples of students' work and teachers' observations.

SELF-TEST

1. Why is it not valid to draw conclusions about a kindergartner's writing development based on the analysis of a single writing sample?

2. Explain why sharing of writing is important. Tell when, during the process, sharing may profitably take place, what forms it may take, and what children are likely to gain from it.

3. Define each of the five components of the writing process.

4. Compare the writing process of a first-grader and a fifth-grader. What will be the same? What will be different?

5. Why is it not advisable for a novice teacher to use a list of "canned" minilessons? What is the basis on which good minilessons are developed, and what are their characteristics?

BIBLIOGRAPHY

Atwell, N. (1987). *In the middle: Writing, reading and learning with adolescents.* Portsmouth, N.H.: Boynton/Cook.

_____ (1988). Making the grade: evaluating writing in conference. In Newkirk, T. and N. Atwell (eds.), Un*derstanding writing* (2nd ed.). Portsmouth, N.H.: Heinemann.

Brett, J. (1989). *The mitten.* New York: Putnam.

Calkins, L. (1986). *The art of teaching writing.* Portsmouth, N.H.: Heinemann.

_____ (1991). *Living between the lines.* Portsmouth, N.H.: Heinemann.

Collins, P. (1990). Bridging the gap. In Atwell, N. (ed.), *Coming to know.* Portsmouth, N.H.: Heinemann.

Cowley, J. (1986). *The big toe.* Aukland, New Zealand: Shortland Publications.

Graves, D. (1983). *Writing: teachers and children at work.* Portsmouth, N.H.: Heinemann.

Hilliker, J. (1988). Labeling to beginning narrative: four kindergarten children learn to write. In Newkirk, T. and N. Atwell (eds.), *Understanding writing* (2nd ed.). Portsmouth, N.H.: Heinemann.

Karelitz, E.B. (1988). The rhythm of writing development. In Newkirk, T. and N. Atwell (eds.), *Understanding writing* (2nd ed.). Portsmouth, N.H.: Heinemann.

Morrow, L. (1989). *Literacy development in the early years.* Englewood Cliffs, N.J.: Prentice Hall.

Newman, J. (1984). *The craft of children's writing.* Portsmouth, N.H.: Heinemann.

O'Donnell, M. and Wood, M. (1992). *Becoming a reader: a developmental approach to reading instruction.* Boston: Allyn and Bacon.

Sowers, S. (1988). Reflect, expand, select: three responses in the writing conference. In Newkirk, T., and N. Atwell (eds.), *Understanding writing* (2nd ed.). Portsmouth, N.H.: Heinemann.

Sulzby, E. (1985). Kindergartners as writers and readers. In Farr, M. (ed.), *Advances in writing research, Vol. 1: Children's early writing development.* Norwood, N.J.: Ablex.

Sulzby, E., Barnhart, J. and Heishima, J. (1989). Forms of writing and rereading from writing: a preliminary report. In Mason, J. (ed.), *Reading/writing connections.* Boston: Allyn and Bacon.

Tompkins, G. and Hoskisson, K. (1991) *Language arts content and teaching strategies* (2nd ed.). New York: Macmillan.

Viorst, J. (1972). *Alexander and the terrible, horrible, no good, very bad day.* New York: Atheneum.

Wood, M. (1991). A study of the writing and rereading behaviors of five and six-year-olds. Paper presented at New England Educational Research Association Conference, Portsmouth N.H.

6 Teaching the Conventions of Writing

LOOKING AHEAD

Chapter 5 focused on the composition process and how it develops in children. In this chapter we will give attention to the form of children's writing. Our goal is to help our students develop into writers who not only have the ability to articulate their thoughts in writing, but also have the ability to present them in increasingly correct form, using legible penmanship, standard spelling and punctuation, and correct grammatical constructions. Following an introductory discussion of the issues in teaching writing conventions, we focus on handwriting. The forms of writing usually taught in elementary school are *manuscript* and *cursive*. Developmental and pedagogical factors influence our teaching of penmanship, and we must always keep it in perspective, remembering that handwriting is a tool for composition.

The next part of the chapter is devoted to spelling development and instruction. Most teachers find the teaching of spelling to be problematic for a number of reasons. You will learn what is known about the way standard spelling is learned by writers, and what the options are for facilitating and evaluating spelling growth within the writing process.

The last section of the chapter focuses on what is commonly referred to as "grammar." Once grammar is defined as the analysis of language constructions, we see that its study is not generally useful or appropriate for elementary school students. Punctuation and usage of standard sentence constructions, on the other hand, are very important and teachable at this level in the context of strong reading and writing programs.

CAN YOU?

1. Explain why students' writing development may be impaired by premature emphasis on correctness of form?

2. Give several suggestions for helping left-handed writers learn to write legibly and fluently?

3. Give a rationale for including spelling in the writing program rather than treating it as a separate subject?

4. Describe the four major elements that should be included in classroom practice to promote spelling growth?

5. Explain the difference between grammar and usage?

In controversies about how best to teach conventions of writing, language arts teachers are often caught in the middle. While there is unequivocal research evidence that formal analytical grammar instruction and traditionally taught spelling do not improve students' writing (Cazden, 1972; Shaughnessy, 1977; Smith, 1982; Calkins, 1986), it is obvious that in the real world, correctness of writing *does* matter. It is a measure of literacy by which one is often judged in higher education, in competition for jobs, and in the work place. Realizing this, parents, principals, school boards, and even students themselves want teachers to teach conventions. Adults tend to remember how writing conventions were taught when they were in school—generally through direct instruction and lots of exercises—and expect their children's teachers to address conventions in the same ways.

The question that confronts today's elementary teachers is not whether to teach writing conventions, but rather how to do this. The old methods were not consistently successful and generally were practiced at the expense of time spent on meaningful composition and response. We cannot ignore the research findings on the ineffectiveness of "skill drill" instruction in penmanship, spelling, punctuation, and grammar. We must find ways to effectively help students improve the form of their writing without allowing concern for form to drive the writing program. Today's teachers need to understand (1) how standard forms of writing develop as a part of children's growth as written language users, (2) how to integrate instruction in use of conventions into the writing process, and (3) how to achieve a balance in emphasis between form and content of writing.

What do we know that can help us teach conventions appropriately? Lucy Calkins (1986) reminds us that the assumption that students need to "learn the basics" of written language construction before they are encouraged or required to compose much actually has the reverse of the intended effect. Control of the "basics" is delayed or prevented. In her words, "The infrequency with which students write is a major reason for their problems with mechanics and spelling. Writing is an alien activity for many people" (p. 197). Teachers of remedial writing at the college level note that basic writers have been using oral language effectively in many situations on a daily basis throughout their lives; however, they have written infrequently, and usually under intimidating conditions (Shaughnessy, 1977). The research of Graves (1983) and many others has shown that children's syntax, spelling, punctuation, and penmanship all improve as their overall literacy develops through many opportunities to read and write, even in the absence of direct instruction. Therefore it is universally recommended that we have children write often and that we convey confidence in their ability to write. Calkins (1986) calls this the most important thing we can do to improve the form of students' writing.

Given that students have frequent occasions to write, their form will improve more noticeably and faster if matters of form are addressed in systematic and appropriate ways. Within the writing process, focus on conventions usually occurs in minilessons or during editing. In either case, children need to be reminded that editing will take place after drafting. Concern about correctness during composition distracts the writer's attention from the message, the content of the communication. As Frank Smith (1982) explains, in *Writing and the Writer,*

> If we are struggling for ideas, or for particular words or constructions, or if our thoughts are coming too fast, then the quality of our handwriting or typing, spelling or punctuation

is likely to decline. If we concentrate on the transcription or appearance of what we write, on the other hand, then composition will be affected (p. 21).

All this is not to say that all children will learn to write correctly through osmosis. While lots of meaningful writing experience and incidental learning are major contributors to mastering the conventions of written English, there is a definite need for correct form to be addressed in its own right. Editing may well be left until last, but it is important that it not be left out altogether.

HANDWRITING

The first thing to remember about handwriting is that it must be kept in perspective. *Writing* is the substance or content of composition; *handwriting* is the formation of symbols on paper by the writer. Donald Graves (1983) captures the relationship between the two:

> Handwriting is the vehicle carrying the information on its way to a destination. If it is illegible the journey will not be completed. Handwriting, like skin, shows the outside of the person. But beneath the skin beats the living organism, the life's blood, the ideas, the information (p. 171).

The increasing availability of word processors is a boon to all writers, but particularly to those students who have real difficulty developing transcription skills. Nevertheless, there are still many instances when students (and adults, for that matter) have to rely on handwriting for communication and composition. In order to convey their messages efficiently and effectively, students need to develop legible, fluent handwriting. This is best accomplished through a combination of lots of functional writing experience and regular, short sessions of direct instruction and guided practice.

Forms of Handwriting

Two forms of handwriting are currently taught and used in American elementary schools: *manuscript* (or printing) and *cursive* (or connected script). Students in the primary grades typically learn

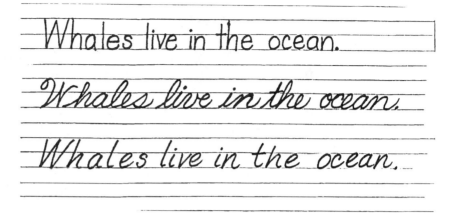

Figure 6-1 Manuscript, Cursive, and D'Nealean Manuscript

manuscript and switch to cursive in late second or third grade. Manuscript is the preferred form for young children because it is easier to learn to produce and to read than is cursive (Koenke, 1986). Since the forms of manuscript letters in handwriting and in the typeset letters in the books children encounter are nearly identical, there is consistent reinforcement of the same forms.

Even after children have learned cursive, manuscript writing should remain an option. Research does not support the common assumption that cursive is more rapidly produced than manuscript. Preference seems to be an individual matter among those who have learned both forms; many older children and adults actually prefer manuscript or their own unique combinations of the two forms. The reasons for teaching and urging students in upper elementary grades to use cursive writing have more to do with tradition than with proven advantages (Koenke, 1986). Young children often see cursive as a "grown-up" form of writing and are therefore eager to learn it. For others, however, cursive represents a whole new form of writing imposed on them just as they are beginning to master the manuscript form. For them the switch is difficult and frustrating, and we must ask ourselves if it is really necessary.

In 1968 Donald Neal Thurber, a teacher in Michigan, developed and publicized a new manuscript and cursive handwriting style which he called D'Nealian. In D'Nealian manuscript the letters are slanted and always formed with a continuous stroke. The style of the D'Nealian cursive form is simplified; the letters lack the flourishes of traditional cursive. The system is designed to ease the transition from manuscript to cursive handwriting and to make legibility and fluency easier for students to attain. Research has not shown any clear advantage to using D'Nealian over traditional forms of the manuscript and cursive alphabets, however (Trap-Porter et al., 1984).

Handwriting Instruction

Handwriting instruction must be linked with functional, purposeful writing at all grade levels, beginning in kindergarten. Most kindergarten teachers focus on teaching children to form upper and lower case letters and to print their names. Kindergartners write labels and messages, accompany their drawings with print, and write in journals. They need to know how to hold writing utensils, how to form letters, and eventually how to space letters and words. Practice with standard formation of letters will promote eventual fluency. Kindergartners enjoy practicing not only with pencils and pens, but also with paints and brushes or in finger paint.

Formal handwriting instruction generally begins in first grade. Contrary to popular belief, young children do not need to write with special "fat" beginners' pencils. They prefer regular pencils (with erasers) and are not generally helped by "grip aids" that slip onto the pencil. An interesting finding about writing utensils is that by third grade most children produce longer pieces of writing when using felt-tip or ballpoint pens than when using pencils (Askov and Peck, 1982).

A variety of kinds of lined and unlined paper are found in elementary classrooms. Early childhood educators often recommend that unlined paper be used in kindergarten. Most primary-grade teachers prefer that their students use lined paper for handwriting activities, but there is no concensus on the value of various line intervals. Children seem to adjust to whichever type of paper is available, sometimes making lines with rulers on unlined paper and at other times ignoring the lines on lined paper when writing or drawing. Teachers need to be sensitive to the fine motor skills of their students and vary the paper used according to the individual needs and preferences of their students, particularly in the primary grades.

Handwriting is best taught in short (15- to 20-minute), frequent (several times a week) periods of direct instruction and guided practice. In kindergarten and first grade, when manuscript forms are being learned, and in third grade, if cursive is being taught, regular periods of penmanship instruction are recommended (Tompkins and Hoskisson, 1991). In the upper elementary grades, occasional reviews of handwriting forms are usually conducted; specific difficulties that individual students demonstrate in their handwriting are addressed with them privately.

During handwriting instruction, it is important for teachers to demonstrate the application of a particular skill by using the board or overhead projector so that all students can observe letter formation. It is helpful if the teacher describes the skill as it is performed. For example, as a first-grade teacher demonstrates the formation of a lower case manuscript *b* she might say, "I start at the top and draw a straight line all the way down to the base-line. Now I go up and around to make the circle part, around, around, all the way back to my line and close it." She demonstrates several times and then circulates among the students as they practice the skill, helping those who need it. This is likely to be far more effective than giving children a sheet of properly formed *b*'s and asking them to trace or copy them. Moving models (students observing the writing as it is being generated and explained) are of greater value to pupils than copying previously written models (Wright and Wright, 1980).

Once students have learned to form letters through this type of brief, guided instruction, practice should take the form of real, purposeful writing activities. It is unrealistic to demand that students' writing always reflect the very best penmanship of which they are capable. Rough drafts of compositions are called "sloppy copies" in some classrooms, because the writer's focus should be on content during the drafting process. The form of the writing only needs to be legible to the writer herself when she goes back to reread it. However, there are times in the writing process when the content of the writing is complete and the student can concentrate appropriately on form, producing a final draft for sharing or publication. Sometimes first drafts must be readable by others, as in the case of learning logs, dialogue journals, or notes to others in the class.

Special writing activities that draw attention to the aesthetics of the written product can be incorporated in the upper elementary grades. In one fourth-grade class, a parent who was a calligrapher brought in a felt-tip calligraphy pen for each student and taught the children how to form letters in this special way. She left a calligraphy book in the classroom, and the teacher set up a calligraphy center where children could go to practice this artful form of writing and create "special" documents. In another elementary school, the fourth- and fifth-grade teachers got together one day during summer vacation and wrote favorite short poems and sayings on cards, using various styles of writing. They decorated many of the cards with colorful borders and laminated them. During the school year, their students used the cards to copy poems or sayings that they chose, decorating them appropriately and keeping their individual collections in binders, which they called their Copy Notebooks. Many students developed their notebooks further by carefully copying favorite passages from books they were reading or poems they came across in literature study.

Left-handed Writers

Physical orientation during writing is not the same for left-handed writers as it is for right-handed writers. Students who are right-handed pull toward their bodies as they write; left-handed students, in contrast, push away from their bodies with their hands. They move their writing hand across their writing, often covering what they have just written. Left to their own devices, many children avoid this by adopting a "hook" position which keeps their left hand above their writing. This can make writing awkward and tiring for them.

Teachers can help left-handed students to make adjustments in how they grip their writing utensils, how they position writing paper, and how they slant their writing, to make writing less cumbersome and more legible. First, left-handed children should be encouraged to hold their pens or pencils about an inch further back from the tip than right-handers. This prevents writing from being covered by the hand or smudged during writing. Left-handers need monitoring and reminders not to "hook," but rather to keep their wrist straight and their elbow close to the body. Some teachers maintain that practice on the blackboard helps left-handed youngsters to maintain the correct hand position and develop a comfortable, legible style.

Left-handed students should tilt their paper slightly to the right, unlike their right-handed peers, whose paper tilts to the left. Whereas right-handed students are encouraged to slant their cursive letters to the right, left-handed writers generally write vertically or with a slight backward slant. Such adaptations should be not only allowed, but also encouraged, to prevent handwriting difficulties.

Handwriting instruction is a very small part of a sound language arts program. Teachers who have penmanship in the proper perspective are always aware that legibility and fluency are the goals of attention to penmanship, and that legible writing is simply a tool with which the writer conveys ideas.

SPELLING

Spelling is perhaps the most problematic writing convention for many teachers. It is all very well to encourage invented spelling by young writers producing drafts, they say, but how do we help them move toward conventional spelling as they progress through the grades? Upper elementary-grade teachers see wide differences in individual students' ability to spell conventionally, as well as in their attitudes toward the importance of "correctness" and toward themselves as spellers. Historically, teachers have assigned weekly lists of words to be memorized, tested students' ability to write these words (generally in list form) correctly at the end of the week, and given separate grades in spelling based on these activities. Research has shown that reliance on this method of teaching spelling is generally not effective in improving students' spelling in the context of composition (Gentry, 1987). Experienced teachers have known this for a long time. They are frustrated when they see students get 100% on weekly spelling tests, yet spell the same words incorrectly in compositions. And then there are always students who can't seem to memorize spellings sufficiently well to pass the Friday tests. But what is the alternative to list-study-test instruction?

First, let us look at some truths about spelling. Standard spelling is a convention, observed out of politeness to the reader. The content of a piece of writing, of course, is its most important aspect. If the author's spellings are far enough from standard, however, the poor spelling may prevent the reader from understanding the message. In less serious cases, non-standard spellings distract the reader from the message. We know that overemphasis or premature emphasis on correctness of spelling can literally cripple young children's efforts to write, since the task of spelling the words they wish to use is so daunting. Afraid of errors, they may stick to those words they know they can spell correctly, thus greatly inhibiting their writing. If, on the other hand, correctness of spelling is entirely ignored, or if all editing is done for students for many years, they develop a cavalier attitude toward spelling and do not move toward conventionality as soon or as well as they might. Our goal as teachers is to give spelling an appropriate emphasis *within the writing program* and to help children take increasing responsibility for standard spelling as they gain proficiency as writers.

The research on effective teaching and learning of spelling is often conflicting and confusing in regard to methods and materials. The use of weekly lists of words from spelling texts or workbooks, to be practiced and memorized (often in groups related by spelling patterns), is still widespread. Claims are made about the relative effectiveness of various techniques for mastering spellings. Many teachers have responded to the admonitions of writing researchers that spelling study should evolve from students' writing (rather than from a preordained spelling curriculum), by generating lists of spelling words from the misspelled words in students' drafts. Such lists may be highly individualized (requiring skillful management of spelling instruction by the teacher); nevertheless, the goal is still for children to memorize the spellings and prove their mastery by writing lists of words correctly on tests. Teachers who wish to treat spelling as a part of the writing process and not as a separate subject or competency incorporate spelling in editing conferences and minilessons (see chapter 5) and do not give spelling tests or separate grades in spelling. The research on writing process supports their practice, they maintain. And yet, coming out of any and all of these different programs we have some older students who are excellent spellers and others whose spelling is "atrocious" by the standards of their English teachers. Among any group of educated adults (including students in teacher education programs) there are good spellers and comparatively poor spellers, most of whom have learned to compensate for their weakness through various editing techniques.

Spelling Development

We know that spelling, like all aspects of language, is developmental. During their early years as writers and readers children approximate spellings of words. As they gain experience, their spellings become closer and closer to conventional forms. In chapter 5, you were introduced to emergent writing and the forms of writing used by very young children. Researcher Richard Gentry has further delineated stages of spelling development that begin at the point when children use letters and letter-like forms to represent writing. Knowledge of these predictable stages is useful for teachers.

Precommunicative spelling consists of strings of letters and letter-like marks (and sometimes numbers as well) chosen at random and is equivalent to Sulzby's "Letter Strings" (see chapter 5). At this stage the child uses the letters she knows how to write, with no regard to letter-sound correspondence. The alphabetic principle (letters stand for speech sounds) is either not yet understood or not yet consistently used. For example, a precommunicative speller might represent "I like to ride my Big Wheel" as FJSOSOTFS.

Semiphonetic spelling is generated from some knowledge of letter-sound correspondences, but the sounds in words are only partially perceived and represented. A semiphonetic speller might write I L t RD M B WL for "I like to ride my Big Wheel." Remember that emergent writers may switch back and forth between precommunicative and semiphonetic spelling, depending on what they are attempting to record.

Phonetic spelling is the term used by Gentry for spellings that include all the speech sounds in words, recorded as the child hears and represents them. "I like to ride my Big Wheel" might be represented as I LiK 2 riD mi BEG weL. Truly phonetic spellers' basic strategy is to spell words the way they pronounce and hear the words. Their mapping of symbols to sounds is systematic and logical.

Transitional spelling consists of a mix of conventional and phonetic spelling elements. The transitional speller has begun to read conventionally and develop sight vocabulary, and has begun to rely on visual memory as well as phonetic strategies. She understands that all standard spellings are not entirely phonetic. She might write "I like to rid mie Big Wele." Silent *e*'s, vowel digraphs, and non-phonetic combinations such as *gh* appear, often where they are not actually used in standard spelling. (My favorite exotic spelling is a second-grader's *highcked* for "hiked.")

Mature spelling is for the most part conventional, or "correct," spelling. The mature speller understands the basic rules of the English spelling system, knows how to distinguish most homonyms, uses silent letters and double consonants correctly, has mastered many irregular spellings, recognizes meaning connections between words and uses this information to spell correctly, and is accumulating a large number of known, "automatic" spellings (Gentry, 1987; Wood, 1982).

Children who are encouraged to spell independently and who are immersed in meaningful reading and writing experiences generally pass through the first four of these stages between ages four and eight. In the earliest grades, then, the best thing we can do for children's spelling development is to give them daily opportunities and motivation to write, encouraging them to use whatever strategies they have to spell on their own, and helping them further develop these strategies. When adults spell for them and they copy standard spellings, they are not learning about writing. Learning to write and spell is an active, constructive process. While inventing spellings, children think about words and generate new knowledge about the relationship between speech and print. In grades K and 1, purposeful writing and our acceptance of that writing is probably the most important key to spelling development. In addition, of course, children in those grades should be exposed to conventionally spelled words in the print materials in their environment.

Spelling Instruction

Formal spelling instruction, if it is to be undertaken, is not recommended until second grade. Regardless of what kind of writing/spelling instruction is experienced, some students will progress much faster and more easily than others from transitional to mature spelling. Proficient spellers depend largely on visual memory of word forms; they have a sense of which spellings "look right." While extensive exposure to standard spellings (through wide reading and careful editing of writing) is a necessary condition for spelling development (Krashen, 1989), individuals' ability to remember the visual forms of words varies and ultimately plays a major role in determining the ease or difficulty with which they progress toward mature spelling. Henderson (1990) maintains that achieving spellers gradually internalize the "ordering principles" of English spelling (likely vowel combinations, for example), which reduces the load on memory. Nonachieving spellers, in contrast, continue to spell by sound "and the tattered remnants of what they tried to remember but partially forgot" (Henderson, 1990, p. 90). In order to become proficient at English spelling, it is necessary to have constant exposure to exemplars of conventionally spelled words as well as regular opportunities to give close attention to spellings of words and to compare one's attempts to correct models. In other words, spelling (unlike proficient reading) requires attention to the structure of words at the letter-level.

Sandra Wilde, a researcher with a particular interest in spelling, reminds us that spelling should not be seen as a "subject," but rather as a language system that is learned through use. She believes that classroom practice should include four major elements: providing opportunities for learning, supporting learning, influencing beliefs and attitudes, and evaluating (Wilde, 1990).

Opportunities to Learn

Spelling is a component of written language that develops in an environment that includes frequent exposure to writing and opportunities to use writing for real purposes. In such an environment, learning about written language takes place constantly, with or without teaching. Such learning includes a process (often not conscious) of making and testing hypotheses about the way English spelling works, as well as familiarity with individual words. It is through this process that a transitional speller comes up with an invented spelling such as MIE for "my," which shows understanding of the function of the silent *e.* Classroom practices that expose children to print facilitate the development and testing of hypotheses about the English spelling system. First and foremost, wide reading is recommended. It is also important for the classroom to contain resources for children to use when they need to find conventional spellings of words they wish to use in writing. Wall charts are an important resource, particularly in the primary grades. They can contain high-frequency words or words particular to seasons, events, or content-area study. Many second and third grade teachers have "word walls" in their classrooms. Words are grouped in lists headed by such titles as *Common Words, Dinosaurs, Halloween Words, Months, Days of the Week,* and *Fairy Tale Characters.* Students may use these references in first-draft writing, as an alternative to inventing a spelling, but the lists are more commonly used as a resource in proofreading and editing in preparation for final drafts or publishing. Children are not necessarily expected to memorize or "master" the conventional spellings of these words; rather, they learn to use these resources for independent correction of spellings, and in the process are exposed to more and more standard spellings.

The more obvious reference tools for spelling, dictionaries and thesauruses, should be available to writers. Wilde (1990) recommends a variety of references rather than class sets of a single dictionary. Picture dictionaries, different children's dictionaries, adult dictionaries, poor spellers' dictionaries, and encyclopedias are all useful to children as spelling references.

Of course, students can only test out their strategies for spelling when they are actually writing, so regular, frequent writing is crucial to spelling development, as we have already seen.

Supporting Learning

Teachers need to do more than provide opportunities for children to explore spelling on their own; they can promote spelling and proofreading strategies and actively help children discover spelling rules and generalizations that are consistent enough to be helpful. The process of "what can you do when you don't know how to spell a word" should be explored thoroughly with children. In the past, students were usually told to look up unknown words in the dictionary, but in fact this is probably the strategy least used by adults, and it is difficult or impossible to do unless one's spelling guess is reasonably close to the conventional spelling. There are a variety of other strategies for generating spellings of words while drafting. It probably makes most sense to try first those strategies that do not depend on outside resources, since stopping to look words up interrupts the flow of writing. Students can share the strategies they use, such as sounding out, thinking of related words, or thinking about the parts of words, to determine how a word might be spelled. Good spellers often write more than one possible spelling of a word to see which one "looks right." Children can add this to their repertoire of strategies. Sixth-grade teacher Victoria Perry and her students developed the following list of strategies:

1. Ask someone. (Know who to ask!)

2. Look it up in the dictionary.

3. Look it up in the thesaurus.

4. Look it up in the spelling dictionary.

5. If you are using the computer, use the spell checker.

6. Write it a few times to see which way looks the best.

7. Is it written in the room somewhere?

8. Is it in the book you are reading?

9. Use mnemonics (tricks for remembering)

10. Be attentive and interested in spelling. (Perry, 1992, p. 26.)

Development of proofreading skills has traditionally been neglected in formal spelling programs. It is not productive for students to go through exercises that require them to find and correct errors in artificial texts contrived for this purpose. They gain far more by proofreading their own writing. Teachers in the upper grades tend to return student papers with spelling errors marked and often corrected. This practice keeps students dependent on a higher authority for proofreading. The ultimate goal of spelling instruction is the production of polished final drafts in conventional spelling. We work toward this in age- and stage-appropriate ways. For young or unaccomplished spellers who still invent many or most of their spellings, a requirement that they find and correct three or four words in one text might be reasonable. Older, more proficient writers should be able to pinpoint most misspelled words in their text and to correct them using all available resources, before the final draft goes to the teacher. Proofreading and editing ability develop gradually and through practice. Of course, focus on these steps always should come last (or last before publishing) in the writing process.

In addition to spelling strategies, rules and generalizations can profitably be discussed and taught, provided certain cautions are observed. Experts on English spelling agree that there are only a few generalizations that are sufficiently predictable and consistent to be worth teaching (Wheat, 1932; Gentry, 1987; Wilde, 1990). Useful rules include

- the one for determining whether *ei* or *ie* should be used

- those relating to dropping *e,* changing *y* to *i* , and doubling consonants before suffixes

- the rule that *q* is always followed by *u* in English

Spelling textbooks can be a source of rules for instruction, but good judgment must be used by the teacher. Many textbooks present rules that are not predictable enough to be truly helpful. For example, vowel combinations in English are particularly variable. The information on vowel combinations that is presented in spelling texts can only suggest how vowels *might* be used in an unknown word. Knowledge of particular vowel spellings is probably best increased by time spent reading, ensuring exposure to a large number of spellings. It is surely better to choose and teach a few truly useful spelling rules than to clutter students' minds with many that have limited usefulness.

Beliefs and Attitudes

Informed teachers have a responsibility to communicate beliefs and attitudes about spelling that are theoretically valid to administrators and parents, as well as to the students themselves. Learning to spell conventionally is important, but correct spelling is not the be-all end-all of writing instruction that it is sometimes made out to be. First of all, we must remind those who are concerned about spelling that children who mispronounce words while learning to talk are not constantly corrected, and yet their pronunciation eventually matches that of adults. We do not expect learners of golf, chess, or painting to perform perfectly right from the start. Perfect spelling is not an appropriate goal for beginning writers. When they read and write consistently, they grow as spellers. Constant correcting of "errors" or copying of standard spelling inhibits young writers' initiative and prevents them from developing strategies for spelling independently. This information can help parents and administrators understand why teachers allow students to leave misspellings uncorrected and why they encourage invented spelling. Parents can be reassured that their children will not develop bad habits or get "stuck" in invented spellings any more than they got "stuck" in baby talk.

Everyone concerned with spelling also needs to understand that it is very important for children to become independent spellers. Students must know why their teacher usually does not supply correct spellings for them except when publishing. The goal of producing independent spellers helps explain to parents why teachers do not routinely circle or correct misspellings on drafts.

Correct spelling is not a moral issue! For too long it has been considered one of the "basics" of education when in fact it is subordinate to writing, which certainly is a basic. Our goal is for everyone to become able to express themselves well in written language. Conventional spelling is one component of mastery of written language, but only one among many.

Evaluation

Evaluation is not merely a matter of judging competence or performance; more appropriately, it is the assessment of learning, of progress. As stated earlier, the goal in spelling is improvement of spelling in written compositions; thus it is best evaluated through students' compositions. If writing samples are saved, as suggested in chapter 5, teachers can observe the changes in the invented spelling of beginning writers and document increasing ability to proofread and edit spelling in more experienced writers. For more explicit evidence of improvement, writing samples which children have edited to the best of their ability can be analyzed periodically (once every two or three months, for example) to determine the percentage of words spelled correctly. (The number of correctly spelled words is divided by the total number of words written.) Some teachers create a short paragraph containing high-frequency words, words that require use of some of the common spelling generalizations, and phonetically regular and irregular words. They dictate this same paragraph to students at the beginning, middle, and end of the school year and tabulate the percentage of correctly spelled words. These methods of evaluating spelling growth focus on improvement, rather than on individual words mastered.

Many elementary-level teachers are still required to give each student a grade in spelling. If this is the case, care must be taken to grade fairly. Wilde points out that "most spelling grades given in traditional programs probably reflect developmental level and natural ability more than anything else, which is equivalent to assigning grades based on yearly increase in height" (Wilde, 1990, p. 287). Students' levels of spelling and writing maturity and their efforts to improve their spelling in final drafts of written work must be taken into account when assigning grades. If teachers are required to use commercial spelling programs or to base grades on traditional spelling tests, the following procedures are suggested.

- Make absolutely certain that words on spelling lists are within students' reading vocabulary. There is no point whatever in having students try to memorize spellings of words they cannot recognize in context.

- Give a spelling pretest on Monday, have students select from five to seven words that they missed, and encourage them to study these words during the week in any way that works for them. One effective strategy is to look carefully at the word, close eyes and try to visualize the word, cover the word and write it, check spelling against the correct model, and write it correctly if it was misspelled. Some students find it helpful to pronounce the word as they study it, or to say the letters of the word to themselves. It is not helpful to write the word in isolation ten times; this is not conducive to paying close attention to the spelling.

- Have students pair up and give each other post-tests on Friday.

- As an option for good spellers, or as an alternative for all students, five to seven words could be selected from misspellings in their own writings and studied.

The exercises from the spelling book should not be used; they are time-consuming, and students will gain far more from using their time in reading or writing activities. Even the suggested minimal use of spelling lists should be considered as a supplement to a broad, reading- and writing-based spelling curriculum.

Since learning to spell is a developmental process that depends on maturation and experience, pace and direction are ideally determined primarily by the learner. (This is a good example of "responsibility," one of the conditions of language learning described in chapter 2.) In a typical first-grade classroom there are some children using letter strings, others spelling phonetically, and some already knowing the conventional spellings of many words. A typical third grade contains children who invent the spellings of many words, as well as children who spell almost as well as many adults. In most sixth-grade classes, the majority of students spell conventionally most of the time (Applebee, Langer, and Mullis, 1987), but the words they still struggle with vary widely from student to student.

Our goal for children's spelling should be improvement in the proportion of correct to incorrect spelling in their written work, rather than perfect reproductions of memorized words in lists. As we have shown, it is possible to work toward this goal both through discrete spelling instruction, separate from writing, and as an integral part of the writing process, using minilessons, conferences, and editing strategies. Following are descriptions of two teachers' spelling programs which have both proven effective in helping students improve their spelling.

Third-grade teacher Betsy Lane states that a lot of incidental learning about spelling takes place in her classroom through the reading and writing workshops, which include minilessons and editing requirements. She is not comfortable with this as the only avenue for teaching spelling, however. Each week she selects six words that have been misspelled in students' writing and adds four "challenge" words, usually from a content-area unit of study. On Monday she gives a pretest of these words. She presents the standard spelling of the words, and the children self-correct their pretests.

On Tuesday the children review the words and discuss strategies for spelling them and any of the common generalizations that are exemplified in the words. Students enter the words into their "Quick Word Books," self-made spelling references in which words are entered on alphabetized pages. On Wednesday and Thursday children work independently on the list of words, using a Look, Cover, Write (or write and say), Check method. Strategies are often discussed again on Thursday. What have they noticed about the words, and what helped them remember their spellings?

On Friday the words are dictated to students as a test and passed in to Ms. Lane, who records scores. These are considered as a part of students' evaluation in writing when report cards are filled out. (In Ms. Lane's school third-graders do not receive letter grades.) Ms. Lane stresses that she never spends more than 15 minutes per day on this spelling work and that there is no competition between children. She considers this part of her program to be supplemental to the reading and writing workshops.

Sixth-grade teacher Victoria Perry focuses her students' attention on spelling without using lists or worksheets, even though she is required to assign grades in spelling. At the beginning of her first year of teaching sixth grade she administered spelling surveys to see how students assessed their own spelling competence and what their attitudes were toward spelling. She found that many of her students seemed resigned to being poor spellers and felt little responsibility for correct spelling in their compositions. Ms. Perry began a spelling folder for each student. She kept records over several weeks of the words each student misspelled consistently and put them in the folders, along with the surveys. She found that in most cases these lists revealed patterns or certain types of words that individual students were misspelling. She began to work with students during editing conferences on the patterns she had noticed.

Next she inserted a graph into each folder so that students could visualize their spelling progress. Each time a final draft was handed in for final teacher editing, Ms. Perry counted the number of misspelled words and entered the percentage of words that were misspelled onto the graph. The month and type of piece were listed along the bottom of the graph.

She found that the students were fascinated and motivated by the graphs. They consciously used their spelling strategies, learned to figure percentages accurately, and became involved in their own assessment. Spelling on final drafts improved. The students knew that the mandated grade on their report cards reflected their efforts on those final drafts and evidence of improvement of their spelling in compositions. Perry (1992) reports

> By integrating spelling with reading and writing and involving children in their own assessment, my students developed a metacognitive awareness of spelling. When spelling problems arose, they knew there were several ways to find a solution...Putting spelling hand in hand with reading and writing connected things for the children. While they

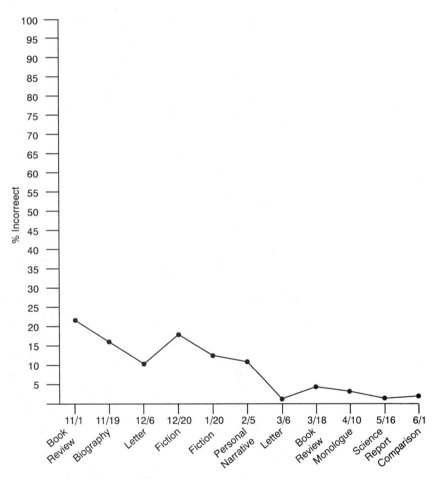

Figure 6-2 Graph Showing Percentages, Correct and Incorrect Spellings

had different problems with their spelling, all the solutions were joint ventures. They learned how to take advantage of multiple resources (p. 24).

"GRAMMAR"

Before looking at the role of grammar instruction in the language arts program, we must define what we mean by "grammar." People often use this term very loosely to include punctuation, correct use of words and sentences, and analysis of the language. The topic becomes less confusing if we separate grammar from usage. *Grammar* is defined by Jean Sanborn (1986) as "the system of rules governing the formation of words and the abstract relationships among words which generates the syntax of the language" (p. 74). *Usage*, on the other hand, is the correct or standard form of the language, accepted syntax, and use of words within sentences. "Grammar is the rationale of a language; usage is its etiquette" (Fraser and Hodson, 1978, p. 52).

As you learned in chapter 2, children acquire the grammatical structure of their native language as they learn to talk. Their knowledge of grammar is implicit. The purpose of genuine grammar instruction is to make this knowledge explicit, to teach students to analyze and label words, sentences, and parts of sentences according to their function. The teaching of grammar has a long tradition in this country. Parents were taught grammar (although few remember much of it) and therefore expect their children to engage in similar study. Teachers who recognize how difficult language analysis is for most of their students rationalize the teaching of grammar on the basis that it prepares students for standardized tests and helps them in the study of foreign languages. A major assumption of the past was that the study of grammar would lead to improved speech and writing. Research over the past fifty years has not supported this assumption, however. Based on an extensive review of the literature on grammar instruction prior to 1963, Braddock, Lloyd-Jones, and Schoer (1963) wrote,

> ...the conclusion can be stated in strong and unqualified terms: the teaching of formal grammar has a negligible or, because it usually displaces some instruction and practice in

actual composition, even a harmful effect on the improvement of writing (pp. 37–38).

Many other studies conducted since 1963 have reached the same conclusion (Mellon; 1969, Elley et al., 1976; Hillocks, 1987). Child language expert Courtney Cazden, of Harvard University, sums up the findings most succinctly of all:

> There is no evidence that learning to be aware of one's tacit grammatical knowledge makes any difference in verbal behavior (Cazden, 1972, p. 240).

Despite the rather unequivocal evidence that grammar instruction is not a supportable part of the elementary language arts curriculum, it remains, probably because the ability to write grammatically is an extremely important outcome of language arts education. If we are to help our students learn what they really need to know without wasting their time in non-productive activities, we must turn again to the distinction between grammar and usage.

Traditional Grammar Instruction

Traditional grammar prescribes the rules for socially acceptable language use. It is rooted in the study of Latin and has contributed labels for parts of speech, parts of sentences, and kinds of sentences. We can use this terminology in discussing language; however, we must remember that the terms and rules that are traditionally taught are not adequate for explaining the workings of the language. The information taught usually includes the following.

Parts of Speech

Grammarians identify eight *categories of words*, or parts of speech, that distinguish the way the words are used in sentences. When you were in school you may have memorized definitions such as "a noun is the name of a person, place, or thing," and "a verb describes action or state of being." Nouns and verbs are essential to sentences. Pronouns may be substituted for nouns. Adjectives modify nouns and pronouns; adverbs modify verbs. Prepositions build upon and modify nouns and verbs. Conjunctions connect individual words or groups of words, and interjections are words that express surprise or strong emotions. If you were like most students, you probably became confused by words like *dream,* which can be used as either a noun or a verb, or by the ways verbs can be used in phrases as nouns (gerunds) or adjectives (participles). Nevertheless you used these words and phrases in your speech and writing and understood them with no trouble.

Parts of Sentences

Independent clauses can stand on their own as complete sentences; dependent clauses, on the other hand, cannot. They modify or replace words in the sentence. Prepositional phrases and adjectival and adverbial clauses are modifiers; infinitives are verb forms but may be used as nouns. With the exception of English teachers and linguists, most of us who have been out of school for a few years have forgotten how to tell these and other parts of sentences apart, and yet we use them with ease, relying on our implicit knowledge of the construction of the language.

Sentences

Remember the definition, "A sentence represents a complete thought"? A sentence has a subject (noun or pronoun and all its modifiers) and a predicate (verb and all its modifiers). Sentences may be classified according to structure or purpose. Structurally, we use *simple sentences*, consisting of one independent clause; *compound sentences*, made up of two or more independent clauses linked by conjunctions; and *complex sentences*, containing one or more dependent clauses. The functional classifications of sentences are *declarative* (those that make statements), *interrogative* (those that ask questions), *imperative* (those that make demands), and *exclamatory* (those that convey strong emotion or surprise).

It is important for speakers and writers of the language to be able to use all of these constructions and others that have not been described here, but competent or even brilliant use of language may be acquired without the ability to analyze and name constructions. If this is true, you may well wonder when or under what circumstances grammar study is advisable. According to Sanborn (1986),

> Grammar is good wine...when we do not serve it before
> its time. When students can not only deal in abstract systems

but can also take the extra step of examining their own unconscious process, then a study of grammar can be a real experience in 'Know thyself' (p. 79).

She maintains that grammar study is entirely appropriate as part of a liberal arts education, but that most students will not benefit from it before junior or senior year in high school. When they are developmentally and experientially ready for it, grammar study is "a way for students to expand their consciousness and increase their awareness of language" (Sanborn, 1986, p. 79). It will not, even at this level, have any effect on the student's writing performance, however.

Instruction in Usage

Unlike grammatical analysis, correct usage must be consistently addressed throughout elementary and secondary school in order for students to gain full command of written English and the societal power that is inherent in that command. (Those who do not demonstrate command of standard English usage are routinely denied access to higher education and to the most desirable, highest paying jobs in our society.) Teachers can address issues of usage through minilessons, which generally involve groups, or editing conferences, which are more likely to be individual. In addition, we must trust that a great deal of learning about usage takes place incidentally if students engage in daily writing throughout their elementary school years.

In 1980, Lucy Calkins conducted a small-scale but interesting study comparing the learning about punctuation that took place in two third-grade classrooms. In one classroom, children learned about punctuation through writing and editing; there were no formal group lessons or drill exercises. In the other classroom (in the same school), mechanics were taught through daily drills and workbooks. The teacher followed the language arts textbook and did a lesson on "everything that is in the book." Children practiced inserting punctuation on sentences she wrote on the chalkboard, and took pretests and post-tests on the forms of punctuation that were taught. The children in this classroom "rarely wrote." Calkins points out that both teachers stated that they "begin at the beginning." For one teacher, "the beginning" was the sentence unit and the rules for using periods and capital letters. For the other teacher, "the beginning" was each child's unique information and validation of her attempts to communicate this in writing. Calkins points out that both teachers "believed in basic skills," but one taught them in isolation, while the other taught them in context (Calkins, 1980).

At the end of the school year, Calkins conducted interviews with each of the children from both classrooms, showing them various punctuation marks and asking them to explain what each was for. She found that the third-grade "writers" who had not had formal punctuation instruction not only used more kinds of punctuation correctly than did their classmates who had formally studied punctuation, but also were able to define or explain more kinds of punctuation (Calkins, 1980). Calkins speculates that in all likelihood the children who viewed themselves as writers and had many occasions to learn about punctuation as they needed it in their own writing, probably noticed punctuation far more than the children for whom it was something learned through drill, divorced from contexts in which they needed it or could experiment with it (Calkins, 1986). This study, along with many, many teachers' observations, points up the effectiveness of so-called incidental learning.

The natural learning that occurs through writing and talking about writing and through guidance in editing can be bolstered by group minilessons. Lessons on usage are different from lessons in grammar in that they focus on correct form, rather than on the rationale behind the correct form. For example, when sixth-grade teacher James D'Allessandro noticed that many of his students were still using the incorrect "Me and ___" rather than the standard "___ and I," he did brief minilessons on three consecutive days. The first day, he wrote two sentences on the board:

Me and Bill went to the game.
Bill and I went to the game.

He underlined "Me and Bill" and explained that many students were writing sentences with this construction. He noted that in standard English (e.g., in books or formal writing), this is considered incorrect; the correct form is "Bill and I." He told his students when in doubt to take away the other name and see how the sentence would sound. Would they say, "Me went to the game," or "I went to the game"?

For the next two minilessons, he wrote five or six sentences on the board, some correct and some incorrect, and had the students identify and "fix" the incorrect ones in unison. This was very effective in helping his students master the correct form of this particular construction. Had this been a grammar lesson, Mr. D'Allessandro would have analyzed the form of the pronoun used and had students distinguish between subjective and objective forms. While some students might have understood such an explanation, it would not necessarily have improved their usage of the forms of pronouns, which is what is most important.

Ultimately it is up to the teacher to decide which grammatical concepts and forms of usage to teach. Those teachers who, because of inexperience, feel the need for guidance in this area, and those who are required by their school systems to use a language arts textbook, can use the book as a source for ideas. Teachers who feel more confident and who are not bound by mandate to use a textbook can identify concepts and forms they wish to teach by assessing their students' writing and noting what kinds of errors in usage they are making. In either case, instruction should be as closely tied as is possible to students' reading and writing; skill worksheets and textbook exercises should be avoided.

LOOKING BACK

In this chapter we have examined the learning and teaching of important conventions of writing: handwriting, spelling, and grammatical usage. All three of these conventions are taught most effectively within the context of meaningful writing for real purposes; drill and exercises should be kept to a minimum. Mechanics of writing may be taught through group minilessons as well as through individual help with editing, and thus naturally be incorporated into writing workshops and writing process. Progress in handwriting, spelling, and usage is to some extent developmental, but appropriate attention and guidance from teachers and peers will maximize students' development. As students progress through the elementary grades, they can be expected to take more and more responsibility for correctness in their final drafts; however, correctness of surface structure should always remain the last step in producing a finished piece of writing and should never be emphasized at the expense of the message.

SELF-TEST

1. Explain the roles that development and reading/writing experience play in learning the conventions of writing.

2. Compare the teaching of spelling as a subject with the teaching of spelling in the context of the writing program.

3. What should our goals for students be in the area of spelling? Explain these goals to a parent who expects to see weekly lists and tests.

4. Suppose you are hired to teach fourth grade. Explain what you plan to do to provide your students with the necessary opportunities and support to learn to spell conventionally.

5. Identify three common problems students might have with punctuation or usage and explain how you would teach this information within the context of the writing process.

BIBLIOGRAPHY

Applebee, A.W., Langer, J.A., and Mullis, I.V. (1987). *Grammar, punctuation, and spelling: Controlling the conventions of written English at ages 9, 13, and 17.* Princeton, N.J.: Educational Testing Service. (ERIC Document Reproduction Service No. ED 282 928.)

Askov, E. and Peck, M. (1982). Handwriting. In Mitzel, H., Best, J., and W. Rabinowitz (eds.), *Encyclopedia of educational research* (5th edition). New York: The Free Press.

Braddock, R., Lloyd-Jones, R. and Schoer, L. (1963). *Research in written composition.* Champaign, Ill.: National Council of Teachers of English.

Cazden, C. (1972) *Child language and education.* New York: Holt, Rinehart and Winston.

Calkins, L. (1980). Research update: When children want to punctuate: basic skills belong in context. *Language Arts, 57,* 567-573.

_____. (1986). *The art of teaching writing.* Portsmouth, N.H.: Heinemann.

Elley, W.B., Barham, I.H., Lamb, H. and Wyllie, M. (1976). The role of grammar in a secondary school English curriculum. *Research in the Teaching of English,* 10, 5-21.

Fraser, I.S. and Hodson, L.M. (1978). Twenty-one kicks at the grammar horse. *English Journal, 67,* 49-53.

Gentry, J.R. (1987). *Spel... is a four letter word.* Portsmouth, N.H.: Heinemann.

Graves, D. (1983). *Writing: teachers and children at work.* Portsmouth, N.H.: Heinemann.

Henderson, E.H. (1990). *Teaching spelling.* Boston: Houghton Mifflin.

Hillocks, G., Jr. (1987). *Research on written composition: New directions for teaching.* Urbana, Ill.: National Conference on Research in English and the ERIC Clearinghouse on Reading and Communication Skills.

Koenke, K. (1986). Handwriting instruction: what do we know? *The Reading Teacher, 40,* 214-216.

Krashen, S. (1989). We acquire vocabulary and spelling by reading: additional evidence for the input hypothesis. *Modern Language Journal, 73,* 440-464.

Mellon, J.C. (1969). *Transformational sentence combining: A method for enhancing the development of syntactic fluency in English composition* (NCTE Research Report No. 15). Urbana, Ill.: National Council. of Teachers of English.

Perry, V. (1992). Teaching spelling with reading, writing, and learner-directed assessment. *Journal of Maine Education, 8,* 22-26.

Sanborn, J. (1986). Grammar: good wine before its time. *English Journal, 75,* 72-80.

Shaughnessy, M. (1977). *Errors and expectations.* New York: Oxford University Press.

Smith, F. (1982). *Writing and the writer.* New York: Holt, Rinehart and Winston.

Tompkins, G. and Hoskisson, K. (1991) *Language arts content and teaching strategies* (2nd ed.). New York: Macmillan.

Trap-Porter, J., Cooper, J., Hill D., Swisher, K. and LaNunziata, L. (1984). D'Nealian and Zaner-Bloser manuscript alphabets and initial transition to cursive handwriting. *Journal of Educational Research, 77,* 343-345.

Wheat, L.B. (1932). Four spelling rules. *Elementary School Journal, 32,* 697-706.

Wilde, S. (1990). A proposal for a new spelling curriculum. *Elementary School Journal, 90,* 275-289.

Wood, M. (1982). Invented spelling. *Language Arts, 59,* 710-714.

Wright, C.D. and Wright, J.P. (1980). Handwriting: the effectiveness of copying from moving versus still models. *Journal of Educational Research, 74,* 95-98.

CHAPTER

7 Children's Literature in the Language Arts Curriculum

LOOKING AHEAD

Children's literature is at the foundation of excellent language arts programs. In preceding chapters you have encountered numerous references to children's literature in general and to individual books. This last chapter provides an overview of what is available to teachers in the way of literature and how it may be used in developing a language arts curriculum. First, the relationship between literature and children's development is examined. This knowledge will help you to be able to select age-appropriate books for the children you teach. Next we focus on children's responses to literature and the importance of validating their authentic reactions to the books they hear read aloud or read to themselves.

Literature is generally classified by genres; the common genre designations are defined and described. Through the content of the literature incorporated into the curriculum, children gain new insights, learn new information, deal with universal issues, and extend their multicultural understanding. Suggestions are made in the last part of this chapter for keeping abreast of new publications and for using various resources to identify excellent books for every-age child and every curricular area.

CAN YOU?

1. Explain what is meant by "the social aspects" of children's literature experiences?

2. List the characteristics of excellent children's literature?

3. Describe nine genres of children's literature?

4. Explain how literature might be used in one of the content areas (such as science or social studies)?

5. Specify several resources for finding the titles of books you might want to use in your classroom or have in your library?

LITERATURE AND THE DEVELOPING CHILD

Bernice Cullinan (1989) defines literature as "all instances in which language is used imaginatively." To Charlotte Huck (1987), literature is "the imaginative shaping of life and thought into the forms and structures of language." Implicit in these and other definitions is the notion of excellence, of lasting value to readers. Our responses to literature stem from our life experiences and our interest in the experiences of others. Writers' skill at creating stories affects the intensity of our response. The literature that "hooks" us, captivating our full attention and interest and transporting us beyond our own daily experiences, is well crafted. The characters are fully developed and believable, the plot is easily followed and plausible, the setting adds to the integrity of the story, and there is a central theme that emerges and gives the story added impact. Words and phrases are carefully chosen for the exactness of their meaning and often evoke powerful images in the reader or listener. Excellent books for younger readers include artistic illustrations that enrich the telling of the story.

Literary experiences are not created by the text alone, however; they are the result of the readers' interaction with that text. Louise Rosenblatt (1978) uses the term *poem* to name the unique construction of meaning from these interactions. The following passage from her book, *The Reader, the Text, the Poem,* describes the transaction between reader and text:

The reader brings to the text his past experience and present personality. Under the magnetism of the ordered symbols of the text, he marshals his resources and crystallizes out from the stuff of memory, thought, and feeling a new order, a new experience, which he sees as the poem. This becomes part of the ongoing stream of his life experience, to be reflected on from any angle important to him as a human being (p. 12).

Children's literature is geared to young readers' social, emotional, and cognitive development. For this reason, it is not enough to identify which books are excellent. We must also ask, "Excellent for whom?" Choosing and helping children choose appropriate and meaningful experiences with literature requires knowledge of child development, as well as knowledge of children's books. Cullinan (1989) points out that children are highly unlikely to read and enjoy certain age-appropriate books after that age has passed. Margaret Wise Brown's *Goodnight Moon,* a comforting story of bedtime ritual that is a favorite of 2- and 3-year-olds, may seem uninteresting to an older child. Maurice Sendak's *Where the Wild Things Are* and Mercer Mayer's *There's a Nightmare in my Closet* deal with common fears of 5- to 7-year-olds, creating central characters who overcome the monsters of their imaginations. The charm and power of these stories may be lost on older children. Eighth-graders are unlikely to be seen reading E.B. White's *Stuart Little* or Laura Ingalls Wilder's *Little House in the Big Woods;* if these books were not part of their elementary school experience, older children may miss them altogether.

There are more than 50,000 children's books currently in print. They are most assuredly not all of equal quality. Thus it is possible that a child might read a great deal and still never encounter truly significant, powerful books. Cullinan goes so far as to say, "...unless children read some of the really good books, they will probably not become lifelong readers" (1989, p. 12). Some children, of course, are guided to these books by parents, other caregivers, or librarians. It is up to teachers to see that *all* school-age children are exposed to really significant books appropriate to their stage of development. The guide to story selection shown in Figure 7-1 will help you to link characteristics of books and examples of stories with the stages of child development you have studied.

Age Characteristics	Story Characteristics	Suggested Books

Infants and Toddlers (Approximatly Birth to Age 2)

Age Characteristics	Story Characteristics	Suggested Books
Explores through senses	Provides tactile, auditory, and visual experiences	*Pat the Bunny* (Kunhardt)
Learns by hands-on approach	Invites participation	*Hand Rhymes* (Brown)
Learns language as label	Patterned language	*Brown Bear* (Martin)
	Brief rhythmic song games	Mother Goose rhymes
	Objects associated with words	*Dressing* (Oxenbury)

Nursery and Early Childhood (Approximately 2 to 4)

Age Characteristics	Story Characteristics	Suggested Books
Builds concepts through direct experiences	Deals with simple concepts	*Shapes, Shapes* (Hoban)
Learns word and thing are different	Identifies objects	ABC books
Sees self as center of world	Focuses on child	*Max's Bath* (Wells)
	Celebrates routine	*Goodnight Moon* (Brown)
Learns language rapidly	Repetitive and rhythmic language	*Millions of Cats* (Gag)
Begins to develop sense of story	Simple plots	*Is Anyone Home* (Maris)
	Structured plots	*The Three Little Pigs*
Sees events as discrete	Cumulative plot structure	*This Is the House That Jack Built*

Early Primary (Approximately Age 5 to 7)

Age Characteristics	Story Characteristics	Suggested Books
Expresses normal fears	Reassuring themes	*Knots on a Counting Rope* (Martin and Archambault)
Develops self-identity	Deals with importance of self	*Dandelion* (Freeman)
Has rich imaginative life	Presents fantasy believably	*Tale of Peter Rabbit* (Potter)
Has developed sense of story	Clear plot sequence	*Rosie's Walk* (Hutchins)
	Predictable plots	*The Three Bears*
Has eye-for-eye morality	Shows justice prevailing	*I'll Fix Anthony* (Viorst)
Develops powers of observation	Gives attention to details	*Who's Counting* (Tafuri)

Figure 7-1: Guide to Story Selection According to Developmental Stage. From Cullinan (1989, pp. 16-17), with permission.

Age Characteristics	Story Characteristics	Suggested Books
Primary (Approximately Age 7 to 9)		
Recognizes differing points of view	Clear identification of point of view	*The Ghost-Eye Tree* (Martin and Archambault
Develops independence in reading	Some easy-to-read vocabulary	*Little Bear* (Minarik)
Prefers realism and law-and-order rules	Realisitc settings and events	*Ramona Quimby, Age Eight* (Cleary)
Recognizes existence of multiplicity of meaning	Multiple layers of meaning	*Frederick* (Lionni)
Begins to manipulate ideas and actions mentally	Characters with whom to identify	*Worse Than Willy!* (Stevenson)
"Conserves," remembers, organizes knowledge	Episodic (longer stories with chapters)	*Charlotte's Web* (White)
Intermediate (Approximately Age 9 to 12)		
Considers alternative realities	Represents alternatives to real world	*A Wrinkle in Time* (L'Engle)
Becomes aware of mortality	Confronts death and other painful issues	*Bridge to Terabithia* (Paterson)
Understands figurative language	Interesting language use	*The Phantom Tollbooth* (Juster)
Understands complexity	Complex plot structure	*The Blue Sword* (Mckinley)
Becomes aware of social injustice	Confronts issues of prejudice	*Roll of Thunder, Hear My Cry* (Taylor)
Generalizes from past experience	Reflects historical conflicts	*My Brother Sam Is Dead* (Collier and Collier)
Develops compassion	Presents emotional and social conflict	*Dicey's Song* (Voigt)
Advanced (Approximately Age 13 and Beyond)		
Accepts responsibilty for behavior	Deals with issues	*Wolf of Shadows* (Strieber)
Appreciates subtle humor	Understated humor	*The Not-Just-Anybody Family* (Byars)
		The Year of the Gopher (Naylor)
Recognizes moral conflicts	Presents moral issues	*The Chocolate War* (Cormier)
Seeks role models and heroes	Biographic material and heroic characters	*Traitor* (Fritz)
		Lincoln (Freedman)
Accepts alternate realities	Offers imaginative fantasy and science fiction	*A Wizard of Earthsea* (Le Guin)

Of course, books are read aloud to children when they are young and are not yet fluent, independent readers. The reading aloud of high-quality children's literature is a frequent (often more than once daily) activity in primary classrooms. Some teachers mistakenly conclude that once children can read well independently, there is no longer any justification for reading aloud to them on a daily basis. In fact, however, the reading aloud to children of excellent books is crucial to students' literacy development through the upper elementary grades and beyond (Trelease, 1985). Reading aloud enables the teacher to expose children to a wide variety of genres and types of literature, to make sure they experience some of the classic favorites for their age and to motivate them to read authors they might not otherwise choose. Many children are capable of understanding and enjoying books that are too long or difficult for them to read on their own. By reading such books to them, the teacher demonstrates the rich experiences that are in store for them as they gain skill at reading.

In addition to hearing good literature read aloud, children need many opportunities to read good books to themselves—books that they have chosen to read. As you may remember from the discussion of literacy acquisition in chapter 2, children develop both skill at reading and motivation to read from having many, many opportunities to read materials they enjoy and to share and extend their reactions to reading through discussions and other follow-up activities. In some classrooms children read books they choose at a designated time several days a week as a supplement to reading instruction from assigned basal texts. There is a marked trend, however, away from dependence on basals and toward "literature-based" programs in which trade books are used in place of basals (O'Donnell and Wood, 1992). (The development and management of literature-based reading instruction will not be addressed in this text because such instruction is within the province of texts devoted to reading methods.) The remainder of the discussion of children's literature in the language arts curriculum applies both to students' own reading and to reading aloud by the teacher.

CHILDREN'S RESPONSES TO LITERATURE

In *Literature and the Child* (1989) Bernice Cullinan stresses the social aspects of children's responses to literature. Teachers need to recognize that all learning occurs in a social context. Experiences and interactions around literature that children encounter through their caregivers and teachers shape their view of literature and its place in their world. As they gain life experience they become increasingly able to take an objective stance toward literature. James Britton (1970) distinguishes between two ways of using language: as a participant (to get things done) and as a spectator. The reader who takes the stance of spectator can observe forms, take note of emotional reactions to reading, and examine literature objectively. One thing that distinguishes older, more experienced readers from younger ones is older readers' ability to view texts as works of art separate and distinct from life (Galda, 1986). Younger readers (fourth- and fifth-graders) tend to base judgements about books on how well the characters and situations reflect their own lives, whereas the older readers (grades 7 and 8) take into account their sense of the author's purpose and the way literature works.

Teachers have more power than many of them realize in influencing children's responses to a given piece of literature and to books in general. Teachers choose the books that will be in their classrooms. They decide upon the ways in which the books will be presented, accessed by children, and used. They demonstrate and encourage appropriate ways of responding to literature, both orally and in writing. Research has shown that the books to which children respond most enthusiastically and spontaneously are those books in which teachers have shown a great deal of interest and approval (Hickman, 1983). Although children generally enjoy well-written books, they also enjoy less well crafted "formula" stories. Most of them prefer fantasy in the primary grades, realistic fiction and mysteries in the intermediate grades, and both reality and fantasy-based stories in middle school and high school (Cullinan, 1989). Teachers sometimes worry that students' tastes in literature are not exactly the tastes teachers are attempting to cultivate in them. Northrup Frye (1964), a well-known Canadian critic, emphasizes that children need to be given time to mature in their reading choices and responses.

> In my opinion value judgments in literature should not be hurried. It does a student little good to be told that A is better than B, especially if he prefers B at the time. He has to feel values for himself, and should follow his individual rhythm in doing so. In the meantime, he can read almost anything in any order, just as he can eat mixtures of food that

would have his elders reaching for the baking soda. A sensible teacher or librarian can soon learn how to give guidance to a youth's reading that allows for undeveloped taste and still doesn't turn him into a gourmet or a dyspeptic before his time. (pp.115-116).

Teachers clearly are influential, however. Through the books they choose to read aloud and share they widen children's interests and stimulate new tastes beyond those children might develop through their self-selected independent reading. While the independent reading of Nancy Drew or Hardy Boys mysteries should not be discouraged, other more complex and qualitative books should be available, read aloud, and made accessible to students.

Whatever the form of response that students are encouraged to use, each child should be allowed and encouraged to give a personal response that is shared in some way with others and to verify or back up interpretations by returning to the text. We should not impose on children our interpretations or judgments of worth of a given book. It is important to listen to *their* responses. We need to provide a rich variety of literary experiences and encourage children to share their genuine reactions to reading, but we must avoid deciding how children should respond or imposing our responses as the "correct" ones. We must put into action our knowledge that readers build their own meanings from texts and that different interpretations are acceptable and expected. The teacher's own response becomes one of many, but a very influential one if it reflects true enthusiasm and genuine enjoyment (Cullinan, 1989).

Student-response activities may be written, visual, or oral. They include *drawings* of favorite parts of stories by the youngest children, *response journals* in which students record responses and comments about the books they read, *dialogue journals* in which children and teachers carry on a written conversation about the children's reading, and *literature circles* (used by Karen Johnson, whose classroom was described in chapter 1) or *discussion groups* composed of students who have read the same book or books that have something in common. Whatever their format, the purpose of response activities is to lead students to reflect on their reading and deepen their involvement with literature. Galda, Cullinan and Strickland (1993) suggest that we refrain from encouraging "over-analysis or time-wasting cute projects; instead, we suggest ways to allow students to live a little longer within the spell of a good book" (p.167).

TYPES OF LITERATURE

Children's books can be categorized in several different ways. In this text we will use classifications based primarily on genre. Books that belong to a certain genre of literature share characteristics usually including overall structure and types of characters, settings, and plot actions. We will include one category that crosses genres: picture books, which share a unique format.

Picture Books

Picture books are characterized by the integration of the story and the illustrations, which are numerous. Plots are relatively brief and easy to follow. Within this format, the content may be realistic, as in *The Snowy Day* by Ezra Jack Keats; fanciful, as in *Burt Dow, Deep Water Man* by Robert McCloskey; or factual, as in *The Milk Makers* by Gail Gibbons. Excellent picture books are appreciated by children and older readers alike for their aesthetic appeal. The integration of simple, interesting text and beautiful artwork make picture books favorites for reading aloud to young children. Because they become very familiar with their favorites, asking to hear them over and over, children gain experience in exploring a book independently, poring over the pictures and approximating the story, "reading" it in their own words or repeating memorized portions of the text.

Picture books are not exclusively used with young children, however. In their book *Beyond Words*, Susan Benedict and Lenore Carlisle (1992) present a collection of articles on the use of picture books with older students.

Folk Literature

Folk literature, or folklore as it is often called, is a broad category that includes folk and fairy tales, fables, myths, and hero tales or "tall tales." These are stories that originated in the oral tradition of a culture and were passed down from one generation to the next; they have no identifiable author. There is some variation in the story depending on who the storyteller is. In recent times, much folk literature has been recorded in writing, but different authors' versions still vary.

Folk and fairy tales, favorites of most children, mirror the values of a culture. They often contain repetitive language and plot elements and heavy use of the numbers three and seven. Characters tend to be stereotypical representations of good and evil. *Hansel and Gretel, Snow White,* and *Beauty and the Beast* are familiar examples of this sub-genre.

Fables are brief tales with a moral. The characters are often animals who represent human virtues and failings. *Aesop's Fables, Just So Stories,* and the stories about Bre'r Rabbit are fables that most American school children hear or read.

Mythology is a special type of folk literature that is full of symbolic meaning. Most cultures have a body of myths that are unique to that culture but that have common themes and symbolic content. They are often explanations for natural phenomena, and they have spiritual content as well, depicting the relationships between humans and their deities.

Legends and tall tales also belong to the folk literature genre. They are often based on a grain of truth or a real person, but they have become greatly embellished and exaggerated in the retellings. The stories of Robin Hood, Paul Bunyan, and John Henry are examples of this type of tale. They use regional settings and dialect and often contain humor. The heroes and their exploits are larger than life, and are loved by children.

Fiction, as a genre, is too broad a category to be useful to teachers or readers in classifying the kinds of stories they choose and enjoy. Therefore we will consider fantasy, science fiction, realistic fiction, and historical fiction separately.

Fantasy

Fantasy is characterized by "imaginary worlds made believable" (Cullinan, 1989). Settings and events are imaginary, created by the author. Animals may think and talk like humans, as in *Charlotte's Web* (White, 1952). Inanimate objects may have the attributes of living things. Time may be manipulated or children may accomplish great feats. Well-written fantasy, however, has an aura of reality that is spellbinding. Fantasy truly stretches children's imaginations and extends their experiences beyond the everyday.

Science Fiction

The most unique feature of science fiction is that it builds stories on an imaginative extrapolation of scientific facts and theories. Science fiction stories are particularly intriguing because of their plausibility. They generally focus on alternate possibilities of the future and incorporate the potential effects, both good and bad, of advanced technology. A popular science fiction book for elementary children is Jill Paton Walsh's *The Green Book*, a story about life and survival on another planet. Madeleine L'Engle's widely read *A Wrinkle in Time* combines elements of fantasy and science fiction.

Realistic Fiction

Realistic fiction stories are set in contemporary times. Characters are believable and events could occur. Elementary-grade students often enjoy reading realistic fiction about children who are a little older than they are. These books allow the reader to enter vicariously into the lives and circumstances of others, broadening their experiences and introducing them to the possibilities that lie ahead in their own lives. Realistic fiction is real in still another way; it is often open-ended. The central character's problems may not all be resolved. Recent realistic fiction reflects an imperfect world (Cullinan, 1989). Katherine Paterson's *Bridge to Terabithia* is a particularly well crafted, realistic fiction book for older children.

Historical Fiction

Stories that belong to the genre of historical fiction are set in the past and feature characters that could have lived at the chosen time and events that could have occurred. Historical fiction is very plausible because it reflects authentic historical knowledge. *Sarah, Plain and Tall* by Patricia MacLachlan and *My Brother Sam is Dead* by James L. Collier and Christopher Collier are examples of historical fiction books that have received acclaim. Because of the natural appeal of stories, children learn (and probably remember) more about historical time periods and events by reading historical fiction than they do by studying texts full of historical facts. Many social studies teachers incorporate the reading of historical fiction into their units of study, much to the benefit of the students.

Biography

The plot of a biography is built around the events of a real person's life. An autobiography tells the story of the author's own life. Laura Ingalls Wilder's *Little House* series would fall into this category. Authors may also choose to research another's life and write a biography, as Russell Freedman did when he wrote *Lincoln: a Photobiography*. Biographies often convey the struggles for survival or success of a strong and interesting character. The fact that they are true makes biographies appealing to young readers.

Nonfiction

Books that are written to convey information and to explain, rather than to tell a story, are referred to as "nonfiction." *Sugaring Time* by Kathryn Lasky and *The Sea Around Us* by Rachel Carson are examples of this genre, which includes picture books, books of facts, how-to books, and other formats for conveying information. All content areas are represented in nonfiction for children: science, social sciences, mathematics, art, music, crafts, and hobbies. Teachers who are planning a unit of study in science, social studies, or mathematics collect good nonfiction books on the topic for children to use as resources. Some of the criteria they use are the dates of publication (to make certain the information is up to date), the completeness, and the accuracy of information included.

Poetry

Poetry is a very special genre. A poem is a message distilled to its essence and written with as much attention to the aesthetics of the language used as to the content. Poetry has meter and rhythm;

sometimes it rhymes, and it usually is filled with imagery. It ranges from nonsensical limericks to deeply powerful expressions of human emotions. In her excellent book on teaching poetry, *For the Good of the Earth and Sun*, poet Georgia Heard (1990) refers to poetry as "painting with words." In classrooms where children are immersed in poetry, where it is made an integral part of the curriculum and the classroom environment, children learn to love it, respond to it, and write their own.

USES OF LITERATURE IN THE CURRICULUM

Through exposure to literature from an early age, children develop a sense of story design and language (see the section in chapter 4 on oral language and literacy). This provides an essential framework both for understanding literature and for writing it. In addition to this, there are several ways in which the content of books may be used to benefit children.

Gaining New Insights

Books are a vehicle for children's exploration of their own thoughts and feelings about life because they provide readers with vicarious experiences of a wide variety of characters, settings, situations, problems, and solutions. For example, when third-grade teacher Mona Gomez shares Byrd Baylor's *I'm in Charge of Celebrations*, her students, who live in New York, get a feeling for the southwestern desert through Baylor's descriptions and Peter Parnall's illustrations. In addition, they are led to think about seemingly small but important events in their own lives that might merit celebration. Authors like Baylor expand and enlarge children's experiences and concepts, as well as entertain them.

Learning New Information

Children who are avid readers are constantly adding to their world knowledge through reading. They learn about the lives of pioneer families from Laura Ingalls Wilder's books. They learn facts about sea creatures from Dethier's *Newberry; the Life and Times of a Maine Clam*. They learn about the underground railway when they read Monjo's *The Drinking Gourd*. The information they gain as a byproduct of reading for pleasure is not acquired in any particular order or sequence. It steadily adds to their store of background knowledge and provides a strong foundation for understanding what is taught in school and encountered in life.

A more planned gathering of information on a given topic occurs when teachers guide children to literature books that will enhance particular units of content-area study. These may be either informational books, fiction, biography, or poetry. For example, when Jean Fontanello's fourth-graders were studying pioneers, Jean read aloud *Sarah, Plain and Tall* (MacLachlan, 1985). She gathered books from the school and public libraries and displayed the collection in a prominent place in the classroom. She introduced the books and encouraged the children to read them for pleasure or for the gathering of information. The collection included Laura Ingalls Wilder's *Little House* series, *The Cabin that Faced West* (Fritz, 1958), *Caddie Woodlawn* (Brink, 1973), *Dakota Dugout* (Turner, 1985), *If you Traveled West in a Covered Wagon* (Levine, 1986), *The Story of Davy Crockett* (Meadowcroft, 1952), *The Story of Daniel Boone* (Steele, 1953), and *Trouble for Lucy* (Stevens, 1979).

Dealing with Universal Issues

Many excellent children's books are about significant issues that profoundly affect the lives of young people. Books about divorce, death, old age, illness, learning problems, prejudice, sex, and drugs are popular with today's youth. Sensitively crafted books on these topics have been written for children of different ages. Such books promote discussion and often help readers to accept and deal with their own experiences and feelings about these issues. After reading Katherine Paterson's award-winning *Bridge to Terabithia*, a group of seventh-graders openly discussed their feelings about the recent death of a classmate a few months earlier. Tomie de Paola's *Nana Upstairs and Nana Downstairs* sparked lively discussion in one second-grade classroom of some of the joys and hardships of living with aging relatives and the difficult reality of losing them. Tommy, the main character in the book, remembers visiting his grandmother, who seemed to always be cooking at the big black stove in the kitchen, and his great-grandmother, who was upstairs in bed. Nana Upstairs dies, and many years later when Tommy is grown up, Nana Downstairs is very old and in bed. She becomes Nana Upstairs, and eventually dies, too. Tommy remembers both of them fondly whenever he sees a shooting star, because his mother told him after Nana Upstairs' death that perhaps a falling star was a kiss from his great grandmother. A story with a similar theme is the poignant *Blackberries in the Dark*, by Mavis Jukes, which is written for slightly older children. It is about Austin's first visit to his grandparents' farm after his grandfather's death. Everything there reminds him of his grandfather, and Austin and his grandmother share their grief. Eventually they begin to be able to see their memories as treasures that will enrich their lives.

Joan Schuchman's book *Two Places to Sleep* became a favorite of seven-year-old Sandra when her parents went through a divorce. First-grader Nicky was drawn to Rosemary Wells' *Noisy Nora* when his baby sister was born. Virtually all primary-grade children enjoy books about siblings, such as Rosemary Wells' *Stanley and Rhoda* and Charlotte Zolotow's *If it Weren't for You*. Books that touch upon the seminal issues of children's lives can have a profound effect on them and convince them of the value and relevance of reading.

The books mentioned thus far are generally not controversial. They may be read to or by children without upsetting parents or other community members. However, books that deal in an explicit manner with sex or drugs often do provoke adverse reactions. Some parents may be expected to object to Beatrice Sparks' *Go Ask Alice*, the diary of a teenager who gets involved in drugs and sex, eventually dying of an overdose. Parents have also been known to object strongly to Norma Klein's *Mom, the Wolf Man, and Me*, because the main character lives with her unmarried mother and the mother's boyfriend. Books such as these that are well written and have an intense appeal for youngsters should be available in libraries for students to select and read; however it is probably not advisable to make such explicit fiction a required part of the language arts curriculum (Hennings, 1990).

Extending Multicultural Understanding

Children growing up in the United States live in a multicultural society. The U.S. has been called a "melting pot," but in actuality our society is far from homogenized. Many of the diverse groups that make up our population retain and pass on unique traditions and experiences. Several major understandings that are necessary for creating a more just and tolerant society can be conveyed and extended through literature. First, literature can convey our common humanity by describing those emotions, needs, desires, and struggles that are common to us all. By building in children a sense of commonality with others, no matter how different they appear to be on the surface, literature helps create resistance to the divisive forces that alienate us from one another.

At the same time, books and stories can illuminate the interesting differences among us, introducing children to the unique cultural histories, traditions, and practices that lend variety and richness to our society. Through literature, children can explore diversity in their own neighborhood, city, and country, and also gain an acquaintance with the larger world society.

Perhaps most important of all, literature can provide a vehicle for developing awareness of the social inequities and forces that impact the lives of individual members of ethnic groups. Non-white minority groups in America are disproportionately victimized by racism and poverty. Literature that focuses on members of these groups brings readers into contact with pressing social issues. As they enter into the lives of the central characters, children vicariously experience the potentially devastating effects of our social structure on the everyday lives of individuals (Bishop, 1987).

As we have noted, children become most intensely involved with reading when they feel a personal connection between the literature and their own lives. Educator Rudine Sims Bishop (1987) points out that the literature we expose children to lets them know who and what we, as adults, consider important and worthy of inclusion. She says,

> Children who find their own life experiences mirrored in books receive an affirmation of themselves and their culture. Children who find that people like themselves are excluded

or denigrated receive another message altogether. They learn that they are not valued members of society and that reading can be a negative or hurtful experience. (p. 61)

Thus it is clearly important for children to have access to and experiences with books by and about African-Americans, Native Americans, Hispanics, and people of Asian origin. Many such books, presenting positive, authentic images, were published during the 1970s. Unfortunately, fewer books about minority cultures have been published since then. There are good quality books about minority cultures available, however. It is up to teachers and school librarians to seek them out.

Bishop (1987) suggests that the upper elementary or middle school teacher who wants to focus with her students on literature about a particular ethnic group might consider beginning with non-fiction to build a knowledge base. For example, Milton Meltzer, who is an historian, has written excellent books for young readers about several minorities. *The Black Americans: A History in their Own Words* consists of excerpts from diaries, newspapers, speeches, and letters—the primary source materials with which historians work—that convey the African-American experience from 1619 to 1983. Other books by Meltzer include *The Chinese Americans, The Hispanic Americans,* and *Taking Root: Jewish Immigrants in America.* Background books such as these can be supplemented with biographies of individuals and followed by folktales, realistic fiction, poetry and fantasy.

Folktales mirror the collective traditions and values of a cultural group, and are typically entertaining stories. Through the reading and study of the folktales of different cultures, students gain multicultural awareness and understanding. Since folktales were usually passed from generation to generation by storytellers before they were ever written down, they lend themselves to being read aloud. It is worthwhile for older elementary students to read and compare folktales from different cultural groups. They may discover common themes, situations, and character types across cultures, while settings may be markedly different.

Realistic fiction, literature that describes life as it is or used to be, is the category containing the most literature about minorities and their experiences. The most compelling and authentic books of this type tend to be written by members of the minority culture being written about. These books have a double benefit. For the children who are members of the same minority group as the author and main character, there is a strong link or sense of commonality between reader and story. At the same time, children who are not from the same cultural or ethnic group the book describes are able to enter into the perspective and relate to the experiences of those who are different from them. Both groups of students are changed by the experience of reading and sharing a good piece of literature. The capacity of literature to change our perspectives can be used by teachers and students to make the world of the future more humane and compassionate.

KEEPING UP WITH CHILDREN'S LITERATURE

There are more than 50,000 children's books in print. Each year 2000 to 4000 new titles are published. Teachers need to be familiar with the resources that are available to help them identify and obtain excellent, appropriate books for their students.

Each year several awards are given for outstanding children's books that have been published in that year. Probably the most prestigious of these is the John Newbery Medal. This award is named for John Newbery (1713-1767) who was the first English publisher of books written specifically for children. It has been awarded annually since 1922 to the children's book deemed the most distinguished contribution to the body of children's literature published in the United States during that year. A selection committee constituted by the American Library Association considers all the new children's books published during the year and selects the winner based on the literary quality of the text. This award has significant educational impact. The winning book receives widespread publicity and is typically purchased by every public library and most school libraries throughout America. A list of Newbery award-winning books may be found in appendix D.

Another well-publicized award is the Randolph Caldecott Medal. Caldecott was an English illustrator who lived from 1846 to 1886 and who is credited with having put "action and liveliness into illustrations for children" (Cullinan, 1989, p. 37). This award, established in 1937, is given annually through the American Library Association to the illustrator of the most distinguished picture book published in the United States during that year.

Several other awards for children's books are given periodically, including:

- The Laura Ingalls Wilder Award, given every three years to an author or illustrator who is considered to have made an outstanding contribution to children's literature

- The Hans Christian Andersen Award, an international award given every two years to a children's author who has made an important contribution to children's literature. An illustrators' award is given as well.

- The International Reading Association Children's Book Award, given to an unusually promising new writer of children's books, based on the author's first or second book

- The National Council of Teachers of English Award for Excellence in Poetry for Children, given every three years to an American poet whose entire body of work is considered to be outstanding

Various lists of outstanding books are published annually and can be of great use to teachers. Every two or three years a comprehensive list called *Children's Books, Awards and Prizes* is published by the Children's Book Council. *Outstanding Science Trade Books for Children* is published every year by the National Science Teachers' Association. The National Council of Social Studies publishes *Notable Children's Trade Books in the Field of Social Studies*.

All of the awards and lists mentioned so far are determined by adults. Of particular interest is a list of books generated by children through the International Reading Association. Groups of children all over the country are given new children's books to read. They vote for the books they like best, and these become *Children's Choices*, published every October in the IRA's monthly journal, *The Reading Teacher*.

Periodicals that review children's literature are excellent resources. *Booklist*, a journal published by the American Library Association, appears twice a month during the school year and once a month during the summer. Books, audiovisual materials, and computer software are reviewed in each issue. *The Horn Book Magazine* is published six times a year and focuses on children's literature. In addition to book reviews, this journal contains articles by researchers, teachers, authors, illustrators, and librarians. *School Library Journal* has a similar content and format. *Bulletin of the Center for Children's Books* is yet another monthly publication. Not only are new books reviewed in the bulletin, they are also rated and labeled as "recommended," "acceptable," "not recommended," and so forth. Approximate reading levels are given, as well as notations about appropriate curriculum areas or topics the book might relate to. *The New Advocate* is a scholarly journal featuring articles that address both children's literature and reading theory and instruction. It is published quarterly.

In addition to these traditional resources for information on children's books, there is a wealth of helpful advice to be found in textbooks on children's literature and in recent books about reading instruction. Regie Routman's books, *Transitions* (1988) and *Invitations* (1991), and Nancie Atwell's popular book, *In the Middle*, contain extensive lists of books and suggestions of literature to use for different purposes and at different grade levels. *Coming to Know*, the collection of teacher essays on integrating language arts with content-area study edited by Atwell (1990), lists books to go with many topics and subject areas that typically interest elementary school students. *The Read-Aloud Handbook*, by Jim Trelease, includes extensive lists of recommended books of all types, with a brief description of each book. These are just a few of the resource books about teaching, written by and for teachers, that suggest specific literature to use throughout the curriculum. Today's teacher has many resources at her disposal to help her place children's literature where it belongs—at the heart of the curriculum.

LOOKING BACK

Children's literature plays a crucial role in the language arts curriculum. Teachers need to be able to distinguish truly excellent children's books from mediocre ones, and know how to match children to age-appropriate books. As children grow and mature, their literature preferences change, and the sophistication and depth of their responses to literature increase. It is important for teachers to allow children their preferences and encourage their authentic responses to literature. The nine genres described help us categorize books and ensure exposure of our students to a wide variety of reading fare. Ideally, literature is used across the curriculum to enhance and enrich students' learning about the world around them and the human experience. Awards such as the Newbery and Caldecott are given yearly to outstanding children's books. There are many excellent resources, including lists, journals, and books for teachers and parents, that we can draw on for ideas about which books to use in the curriculum. Children's lives are immeasurably enriched by literature; it is up to us as educators to ensure that their school experiences include many, many encounters with excellent children's books.

SELF-TEST

1. Give examples of the kinds of books you would include in a first-grade classroom.

2. How would you expect a sixth-grader's choices of books to differ from a third-grader's?

3. Why is it important for teachers not to be critical of their students' tastes in literature? How can teachers influence their students' tastes over time?

4. Design a sequence of literature experiences to share with students who are studying another culture. Explain the rationale for your design.

5. Explain the ways in which children benefit from immersion in good children's literature.

BIBLIOGRAPHY

Atwell, N. (ed.) (1990). *Coming to know: Writing to learn in the intermediate grades.* Portsmouth, N.H.: Heinemann.

_____. (1987). *In the middle: Writing, reading and learning with adolescents.* Portsmouth, N.H.: Heinemann.

Benedict, S. and Carlisle, L. (1992). *Beyond words.* Portsmouth, N.H.: Heinemann.

Bishop, R.S. (1987). Extending multicultural understanding through children's books. In Cullinan, B., ed. *Children's literature in the reading program.* Newark, Del.: International Reading Association.

Britton, J. (1970). *Language and learning.* London: Penguin Press.

Cullinan, B. (1989). *Literature and the child.* (2nd ed.). New York: Harcourt Brace Jovanovich.

Frye, N. (1964). *The educated imagination.* Bloomington, Ind.: Indiana University Press.

Galda, L. (1986). *Children evaluating literature: Patterns of response across grades four through nine.* Final report, The University of Georgia Research Foundation, the Elva-Knight-International Reading Association, and the College of Education, University of Georgia (Athens).

Galda, L., Cullinan, B. and Strickland, D. (1993). *Language, literacy and the child.* New York: Harcourt Brace Jovanovich.

Heard, G. (1990). *For the good of the earth and sun.* Portsmouth, N.H.: Heinemann.

Hennings, D. (1990) *Communication in action* (4th ed.). Boston: Houghton Mifflin.

Hickman, J. (1983). Everything considered: Response to literature in an elementary school setting. *Journal of Research and Development in Education.* 16, 3, 8-13.

Huck, C., Hepler, S. and Hickman, J. (1987). *Children's literature in the elementary school* (4th ed.). New York: Holt, Rinehart and Winston.

O'Donnell, M. and Wood, M. (1992). *Becoming a reader: A developmental approach to literacy instruction.* Boston: Allyn and Bacon.

Rosenblatt, L. (1978). *The reader, the text, the poem.* Carbondale, Ill.: Southern Illinois University Press.

Routman, R. (1991). *Invitations: Changing as teachers and learners K-12.* Portsmouth, N.H.: Heinemann.

_____. (1988). *Transitions: From literature to literacy.* Portsmouth, N.H.: Heinemann.

Trelease, J. (1985). *The Read-aloud handbook.* New York: Penguin Books.

CHILDREN'S BOOKS

Baylor, B. (1986) *I'm in charge of celebrations*. Illustrated by Peter Parnall. New York: Charles Scribner's Sons.

Brink, C. (1973). *Caddie Woodlawn*. Illustrated by Trina Schart Hyman. Riverside N.J.: Macmillan.

Brown, M.W. (1947). *Goodnight moon*. Illustrated by Clement Hurd. New York: Harper and Row.

Carson, R. (1958). *The sea around us*. New York: Golden Press.

Collier, J.L. and Collier, C. (1974). *My brother Sam is dead*. New York: Scholastic.

DePaola, T. (1973). *Nana upstairs and Nana downstairs*. New York: Putnam.

Dethier,V. (1981). *Newberry: The life and times of a Maine clam*. Illustrated by Marie Litterer. Camden, Me.: Down East Books.

Freedman, R. (1987). *Lincoln: A photobiography*, New York: Clarion.

Fritz, J. (1958). *The cabin that faced west*. Illustrated by Feodor S. Rojankovsky. London: Puffin Books.

Gibbons, G. (1985). *The milk makers*. New York: Macmillan.

Jukes, M. (1985). *Blackberries in the dark*. Illustrated by Thomas B. Allen. New York: Knopf.

Keats, E.J. (1965). *The snowy day*. New York: Viking.

Klein, N. (1972). *Mom, the wolf man, and me*. New York: Pantheon.

Lasky, K. (1984) *Sugaring time*. New York: Macmillan.

L'Engle, M. (1962). *A wrinkle in time*. New York: Farrar, Straus and Giroux.

Levine, E. (1986). *If you traveled west in a covered wagon*. Jefferson City, Mo.: Scholastic.

MacLachlan, P. (1985). *Sarah, plain and tall*. New York: Harper and Row.

McCloskey, R. (1963). *Burt Dow, deep water man*. New York: Viking Press.

Mayer, M. (1968). *There's a nightmare in my closet.* New York: Dial.

Meadowcroft, E. (1952). *The story of Davy Crockett.* Illustrated by Charles B. Falls. New York: Grosset and Dunlap.

Meltzer, M. (1984). *The Black Americans: A history in their own words.* New York: Crowell.

_____. (1980). *The Chinese Americans.* New York: Crowell.

_____. (1982). *The Hispanic Americans.* New York: Crowell.

_____. (1976). *Taking root: Jewish immigrants in America.* New York: Farrar, Straus & Giroux.

Monjo, F. (1970). *The drinking gourd.* Illustrated by Fred Brenner. New York: Harper and Row.

Paterson, K. (1977). *Bridge to Terabithia.* New York: Harper and Row.

Schuchman, J. (1970). *Two places to sleep.* Illustrated by Jim LaMarche. Minneapolis: Carolrhoda.

Sendak, M. (1963). *Where the wild things are.* New York: Harper and Row.

Sparks, B. (1971). *Go ask Alice.* Englewood Cliffs, N.J.: Prentice-Hall.

Steele, W. (1953). *The story of Daniel Boone.* Illustrated by Warren Baumgartner. New York: Grosset and Dunlap.

Stevens, C. (1979). *Trouble for Lucy.* Illustrated by Ronald N. Himler. New York: Seabury Press.

Turner, A. (1985). *Dakota dugout.* Illustrated by Ronald N. Himler. New York: Macmillan.

Walsh, J.P. (1982). *The green book.* Illustrated by Lloyd Bloom. New York: Farrar, Straus.

Wells, R. (1973). *Noisy Nora.* New York: Dial.

Wells, R. (1978). *Stanley and Rhoda* New York: Dial.

White, E.B. (1952). *Charlotte's web.* Illustrated by Garth Williams. New York: Harper and Row.

_____. (1945). *Stuart Little.* Illustrated by Garth Williams. New York: Harper and Row.

Wilder, L.I. (1953). *Little house in the big woods.* Illustrated by Garth Williams. New York: Harper and Row.

Zolotow, C. (1966). *If it weren't for you.* Illustrated by Ben Schecter. New York: Harper and Row.

Afterword:
Questions Teachers Ask

Since this text is intended for use in an intensive methods course, the topics of chapters you have read are those considered to be most basic to teaching the language arts. Three important areas of interest and concern which do not fit neatly into any of the book's chapters but which warrant some attention are addressed in this afterword, in the form of answers to questions asked frequently by teachers of language arts.

QUESTION 1

Where do textbooks fit into the teaching of language arts?

Language arts textbooks for elementary school students are used by novice teachers as a source of information about language skills that the textbook authors, at least, deem appropriate for children at a given grade level. They provide models, examples, and practice activities. Many of today's best teachers, however, would say that the drawbacks of textbooks far outweigh their benefits. Textbooks tend to focus on isolated skills that are taught out of context and divorced from meaningful communication. As we have seen, language is learned in the context of purposeful use in authentic situations, not through exercises. Teachers who are required by their school systems to use a textbook or who feel they need the security of one are best advised not to take children through the book from beginning to end over the course of the school year, but rather to use it as a resource for planning instruction or for suggestions that might be helpful in teaching something that has come up in children's oral or written language productions. During Karen Johnson's first year of teaching fourth grade, for example, she reports that she consulted the language arts textbook periodically to get ideas for minilessons and editing tips. She made herself a list of the areas and skills covered in the text, crossed out the ones that she felt were really not appropriate for her students, and checked off the others as they were addressed. She found that most of the "skills" listed were naturally incorporated into the curriculum during the course of the year, although certainly not in the order in which they were presented in the textbook.

One of the problems that teachers face is the difficulty of providing the necessary time for students to engage in sustained reading, writing, and language activities every day. Time spent doing inauthentic skill exercises is too often time taken away from reading, writing, speaking, listening, and examining language in authentic contexts.

QUESTION 2

How are computers used in language arts programs?

More and more schools are providing students with some access to computers, and more and more children are becoming experienced computer users outside of school. Teachers who have computers available in their classrooms face the challenge of finding uses for them that will truly enhance language arts instruction. Computers can be very useful tools, particularly for writing, but they can also be misused.

Word-processing programs are used by many teachers for publishing. Young children's texts can be quickly produced and printed out in edited form, to be bound or mounted and illustrated. Older students can produce their own finished texts on the computer. Children of all ages enjoy learning to use a word processor and composing on it. Once they have acquired some keyboarding skills, older students may revise and edit their writing more frequently and thoroughly on the computer, since it is so easy to add, delete, and move text, as well as to check spellings and change punctuation. The word processor is a particular boon to those children who have special difficulty with legible penmanship. We must remember, however, that the computer is not the answer to problems inherent in composition. In and of itself, it does not cause students to become better writers.

There are word-processing programs designed specifically for children, such as *The Bank Street Writer* (1982, Broderbund Software) and *The Writing Workshop* (1986, Milliken). However, many primary-grade teachers report that their children are perfectly capable of learning to produce text with "regular" programs.

The use of computers in language arts programs is not limited to word processing, although that is the most common application. Data bases can be used to organize and categorize information gathered in preparation for content area-reports (see Figure 4-3), for example. Software programs for use in literature study help students create story maps and present information and ideas gained from reading. Examples of these are *The Literary Mapper* (Kuchinskas and Radencich, Teacher Support Software) and *The Comprehension Connection* (Reinking, Milliken).

There is still a shortage of good software programs that support or enhance authentic language arts instruction. Much of the software available focuses on isolated skill exercises. These electronic workbook activities have all the same drawbacks as their paper-and-pencil counterparts.

QUESTION 3

How does one accommodate children with linguistic differences or special needs in the language arts program?

Most teachers report that one of their greatest challenges in teaching is to provide effective instruction to children who come to them with either "linguistic differences" (they speak a language other than English, or a non-standard English dialect) or particular difficulties in learning to read and write. Let us look first at children for whom English is a second language (ESL). We know that in the process of acquiring their native language, children learn a great deal about the way all languages work. This is true of literacy as well as oral language learning. For this reason, it is often recommended that children receive reading and writing instruction in their native language first. This enables them to translate their skills to English and to acquire proficiency with written English more easily and quickly than their ESL peers who were instructed in English from the start. Unfortunately this option is not often available. Most children with limited English proficiency are placed in classrooms where the teacher does not speak their language and where interpreters are not available. Two general suggestions that will help teachers in such situations are (1) enlist the aid of English-speaking students to help teach newcomers "survival" English ("Hello," "Goodbye," "I need to go to the bathroom"), if needed, and to involve their new peers in games and conversations; and (2) consistently help ESL students to construct meaning from oral and printed language, rather than focus on correcting them. When teachers draw attention to non-standard utterances by constant correction, students tend to refrain from talking rather than be humiliated. This is true of children with non-standard dialects as well as of ESL students. It is far more effective to repeat the student's language in standard form, followed by a question related to the meaning of what the student was saying. Teachers must thoroughly understand that other languages and English dialects that differ from Standard American English are not inferior in any way to our standard form of the language. It is of the utmost importance that we convey acceptance of each student's linguistic and cultural heritage, and that we make as much use as we possibly can of the linguistic strengths they bring with them to school. At the same time, we immerse them in Standard English, demonstrate its use, and instruct them, in appropriate ways, in the use of the forms they need to communicate effectively (see chapter 6, for example, on teaching writing conventions).

Instructional recommendations for young children hold true for ESL students and children with particular dialects, as well as others. Listening to stories read by the teacher stimulates language development and vocabulary growth. Retelling stories is an especially beneficial way to evoke oral language production. Dictated language-experience "stories" and the choral reading of predictable books are also appropriate approaches for all children, but are of special benefit to those with language divergencies. Older children whose command of Standard English is growing benefit from the same process-oriented language arts instruction as their peers, with extra support as needed from fellow students, teachers, and ESL specialists when they are available.

Many of the same recommendations hold true for children who have been classified as learning-disabled, language-delayed, or remedial. Since there is a lack of consensus about what actually characterizes students in these rather arbitrarily assigned categories, our efforts should go into providing appropriate support and instruction rather than into testing and labeling. More and more educators are coming to the realization that all children, with the exception of the few who are most severely handicapped, can learn language. Instead of focusing relentlessly on their "deficits" and what they cannot do, we can revalue them. It is up to us to discover their strengths and strategies as language users and incorporate those as the bases for their further language and literacy learning. The rate at which they progress may be extremely slow, but the pattern of their literacy development is the same as that of students who learn to read and write more easily (see chapter 2). For an extremely informative and practical discussion of the instruction of students with special needs, the book *Readers and Writers with a Difference,* by L. Rhodes and C. Dudley-Marling (Heinemann, 1988) is recommended.

Meaning-based, holistic language arts programs that place an emphasis on teaching language processes and include the kinds of instructional approaches recommended in this text accommodate wide differences in students' competencies and rates of development. While all teachers encounter students with special needs, we do well to remember that what all learners need most is an instructional climate that accepts and respects their efforts, that instills confidence in themselves as learners and as contributing members of their class, and that provides them with real language experiences, both oral and written, that are appropriate to their stage of development. Rates of learning differ widely among individual children, but the conditions for language and literacy learning are the same for all.

A Types of Puppets

Stick Puppets

Perhaps the most versatile and easiest to make, stick puppets are popular. Popsicle sticks, tongue depressors, short dowels, or sturdy straws may be used for the handle. The figure of the puppet that is attached to the stick may be made of oaktag, cardboard, or styrofoam balls. The features of the character are drawn or painted or cut out and glued on the figure, which is the attached to the stick with glue or masking tape.

Cylinder puppets

Cylinder puppets are similar to stick puppets, but they are made from the cardboard tubes from toilet paper, paper towels, or aluminum foil. The various types of tubes are of different lengths and diameters; they lend themselves to different-sized puppets. The cylinders themselves can be painted, and appendages such as construction paper ears or yarn hair can be attached. Construction paper clothing may be glued on. To manipulate the puppet, children insert their fingers in the bottom of the cylinder.

Paper Bag Puppets

Paper lunch bags are a convenient size to use for puppets because they fit the hands of elementary school children. The puppet's mouth is usually placed on the fold of the bag so that children can reach up into the bag, hold their thumb below the fold and their fingers above it, and open and close the puppet's mouth by opening and closing their hand. Facial features and clothes can be painted or pasted on. Ears, arms, and legs may be pasted on as well.

Paper Plate Puppets

The face of a character may be drawn on a paper plate. Other appropriate decorations may be glued on. A stick or ruler is taped to the back of the plate for manipulation.

Finger Puppets

Students can make several different types of puppet that fit on a finger. They can draw and cut out small oaktag or construction paper figures, add tabs to either side of the figure, and tape the tabs together to fit around the finger. They can make larger puppets that can be taped around the whole hand.

Another type of finger puppet is made by cutting the finger from an old glove and decorating it to represent a character. Some teachers cut up egg cartons and use the pointed part that separates the egg compartments to make finger puppets.

Sock Puppets

Old socks make good puppets; they fit easily over children's hands. Features may be drawn on with felt-tip markers or glued on. Buttons may be sewn in place for eyes.

Cloth Puppets

If teacher aides or parents are available to help with sewing (for younger children), students can make cloth puppets. The figure of the puppet is drawn and cut from a double thickness of cloth. The bottom is left open, and the rest of the double cut-out is sewn together a short distance from the edge. (This can be done by machine or by hand.) The puppet is then turned right side out and decorated to represent a character, using fabric scraps, lace, yarn, and whatever other materials are available. Cloth puppets are more elaborate and more difficult to make than the other types of puppets described; they may be more appropriate for upper elementary-age children.

B Directions for making Hardcover Books

1. Fold 12" by 18" piece of white drawing paper in half, to crease. Unfold it.

2. Cut 9" by 12" piece of oaktag in half.

3. Place one sheet of oaktag on each side of white drawing paper, leaving ½" between the pieces of oaktag.

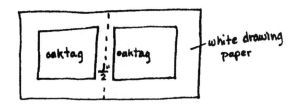

4. Secure oaktag with glue stick (or with photoflat and a laminating machine).

5. Fold margins of paper on four sides to form book jacket. (Margins will be approximately 1" horizontally, and 2½" vertically).

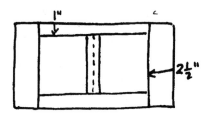

6. Secure margin flaps with glue stick.

7. Stich completed book to construction paper backing, or staple it using long-armed stapler.

8. Glue construction paper to oaktag.

9. After author has lettered and decorated front cover, cover book with clear contact paper. Cut edges diagonally for smooth fit.

C Writing Assessment Checklists

The checklists that follow were designed collaboratively with Marsha Winship, an experienced classroom teacher who conducts action research and leads teacher workshops in addition to teaching a multigrade class. Checklists lose their utility if they become too long and detailed. For this reason we made certain that each checklist contained only essential information and broke this information into categories for assessment purposes. There is a seperate checklist for each stage of literacy development described in chapter 2.

The checklists are intended as guides for assessment of writing growth and are most often used by teachers to summarize and organize the information gleaned from the student's writing folder or portfolio. The format of the checklists provided in this appendix includes spaces to note the dates of evaluation and small boxes in which to record brief remarks or simply check marks. Some teachers prefer to use a seperate form for each evaluation and eliminate the vertical lines on the right half of the page, leaving room for more extensive comments. Others have eliminated one or two of our items and replaced them with items they felt were more important or fitted their students better. This is entirely appropriate, since the checklists are intended only to give teachers a suggested framework for reporting writing behaviors and progress.

You will note that the first checklist, for children in the emergent literacy stage, includes oral language and reading behaviors, as well as writing. The reason for this is that at this stage, all these forms of language development are occurring simultaneously in very interwoven ways. For children in the initial, transitional, and basic literacy stages, it made more sense to have seperate checklists for reading and for writing. (Only the writing checklists are included in this text.) The checklists are purposely not designated for age or grade levels. Teachers are encouraged to identify the stage of each of their students and use the appropriate checklist for that student's current developmental stage.

Assessment of Emergent Literacy

Name of Student_____   Teacher_____

DATE: _____   _____ _____ _____

Oral Language Development				
Retelling Stories (completeness, sequence, characters, details, "story" language)				
Storybook "Reading"				
Book Handling (right side up, spine on left, etc.)				
Distinguishes Print from Pictures. ("What part tells the story"?)				
Attends to Pictures (as cues for "reading" stories)				
Attends to Print				
Writing/Rereading Development				
Form of Writing (drawing, scribble, letter strings, invented, conventional)				
Directional Principles (L-R, R-L, random placement, serpentine, spaces between words)				
Forms of Rereading (label/description, dialogue, speech-like narrative, literature-like narrative)				
Use of Print in Rereading (disregards print, points to and tracks print, uses letter cues, conventional rereading)				
Print Awareness				
Concept of Word, Letter, Sentence (can point to)				
Letter Knowledge				
Sight Word Vocabulary				

Assessment of Initial Writers

Name of Student _____   Teacher _____

DATE: _____ _____ _____ _____

Content of Writing				
Mostly Labeling of Drawings Writes Connected Texts: • Single Page • Several Pages on Same Topic				
Genres (T=tried, P=preferred): • Personal Narrative • Fiction • Poetry • Informational • Other				
Story Structure (narratives): • Events Only • Story Elements (setting, problem, solution)				
Writing Behaviors				
Topics: • Generates Topics • Variety of Topics • Repeats Topic(s)				
Draws, then Writes Writes, then Draws Usual Length of Writing				
Shares Writing With: • Teacher • Peers • Large Group				
Publishes (frequency)				
Conventions				
Left to Right Spaces Between Words Letters (upper case, lower case, random, mix, conventional use)				
Puntuation: • End-Stop • Speech Marks • Apostrophes				
Spelling Strategies: • Letter-Sound Correspondence • Copies from Resources • Some Memorized Words				

Assessment of Transitional Writers

Name of Student_____   Teacher_____

DATE: _____   _____   _____   _____

Content of Writing				
Genres (T=tried, P=preferred): • Personal Narrative • Fiction • Poetry • Informational • Other				
Story Structure (narratives): • Events Only • Story Elements (setting, problem, solution)				
Writing Behaviors				
Topics: • Generates Topics • Variety of Topics • Repeats Topic(s)				
Shares Writing With: • Teacher • Peers • Large Group				
Strategies for Revising Content: • Add On • Insert • Rearrange • Delete				
Pieces Begun/Finished/Published				
Edits for Conventions				
Proofreads Writing				
Punctuation: • End-Stop • Speech Marks • Apostrophes				
Uses Capital Letters Appropriately				
Margins/Paragraphs/Indentation				
Handwriting				

Assessment of Basic Literacy Writers

Name of Student_____   Teacher_____

DATE: _____ _____ _____ _____

Content of Writing				

Genres (T=tried, P=preferred):
• Personal Narrative
• Fiction
   Character development
   Plausibililty
• Poetry
• Informational				

Use of Learning Logs				
Writing Behaviors				
Topics: • Generates Topics • Responds to Teacher-Directed Topics				
Evidence of Planning Writing				
Shares Writing With: • Teacher • Peers • Large Group				
Conveys Information Effectively				
Strategies for Revising Content: • Add On • Insert • Rearrange • Delete				
Pieces Begun/Finished/Published				
Edits for Conventions				
Proofreads: • Detects Missing Words/ Incomplete Sentences • Circles Misspelled Words				
Punctuation				
Correct Usage				
Margins/Paragraphs/Indentation				
Handwriting				

D Newbery Award-Winning Books

1922 *The Story of Mankind*, by Hendrik Willem van Loon (Liveright)

1923 *The Voyages of Dr. Dolittle*, by Hugh Lofting (Lippincott)

1924 *The Dark Frigate*, by Charles Hawes (Little, Brown, Atlantic)

1925 *Tales from Silver Lands*, by Charles Finger (Doubleday)

1926 *Shen of the Sea*, by Arthur Bowie Chrisman (Dutton)

1927 *Smoky, The Cowhorse*, by Will James (Scribner's)

1928 *Gayneck, The Story of a Pigeon*, by Dhan Gopal Mukerji (Dutton)

1929 *The Trumpeter of Krakow*, by Eric P. Kelly (Macmillan)

1930 *Hitty, Her First Hundred Years*, by Rachel Field (Macmillan)

1931 *The Cat Who Went to Heaven*, by Elizabeth Coatsworth (Macmillan)

1932 *Waterless Mountain*, by Laura Adams Armer (Longmans)

1933 *Young Fu of the Upper Yangtze*, by Elizabeth Foreman Lewis (Winston)

1934 *Invincible Louisa*, by Cornelia Meigs (Little, Brown)

1935 *Dobry*, by Monica Shannon (Viking)

1936 *Caddie Woodlawn*, by Carol Ryrie Brink (Macmillan)

1937 *Roller Skate*, by Ruth Sawyer (Viking)

1938 *The White Stag*, by Kate Seredy (Viking)

1939 *Thimble Summer*, by Elizabeth Enright (Rinehart)

1940   *Daniel Boone,* by James Daugherty (Viking)

1941   *Call It Courage,* by Armstrong Sperry (Macmillan)

1942   *The Matchlock Gun,* by Walter D. Edmonds (Dodd)

1943   *Adam of the Road* by Elizabeth Janet Bray (Viking)

1944   *Johnny Tremain,* by Esther Forbes (Houghton Mifflin)

1945   *Rabbit Hill,* by Robert Lawson (Viking)

1946   *Strawberry Girl,* by Lois Lenski (Lippincott)

1947   *Miss Hickory,* by Carolyn Sherwin Bailey (Viking)

1948   *The Twenty-One Balloons,* by William Rene du Bois (Viking)

1949   *King of the Wind,* by Marguerite Henry (Rand)

1950   *The Door in the Wall,* by Marguerite de Angeli (Doubleday)

1951   *Amos Fortune, Free Man,* by Elizabeth Yates (Aladdin)

1952   *Ginger Pye,* by Eleanore Estes (Harcourt Brace)

1953   *Secret of the Andes,* by Ann Nolan Clark (Viking)

1954   *And now Miguel,* by Joseph Krumgold (Crowell)

1955   *The Wheel on the School,* by Meindert DeJong (Harper & Row)

1956   *Carry on Mr. Bowditch,* by Jean Lee Latham (Houghton Mifflin)

1957   *Miracles on Maple Hill,* by Virginia Sorensen (Harcourt Brace)

1958   *Rifles for Watie,* by Harold Keith (Crowell)

1959   *The Witch of Blackbird Pond,* by Elizabeth George Speare (Houghton Mifflin)

1960   *Onion John,* by Joseph Krumgold (Crowell)

1961   *Island of the Blue Dolphins,* by Scott O'Dell (Houghton Mifflin)

1962   *The Bronze Bow,* by Elizabeth George Speare (Houghton Mifflin)

1963   *A Wrinkle in Time,* by Madeleine L'Engle (Farrar, Straus & Giroux)

1964   *It's Like This, Cat,* by Emily Cheney Neville (Harper & Row)

1965   *Shadow of a Bull,* by Maia Wojciechowska (Atheneum)

1966   *I, Juan de Pareja,* by Elizabeth Borten de Trevino (Farrar, Straus & Giroux)

1967   *Up a Road Slowly,* by Irene Hunt (Follet)

1968   *From the Mixed-Up Files of Mrs. Basil E. Frankweiler,* by E.L. Konigsburg (Atheneum)

1969   *The High King,* by Lloyd Alexander (Holt)

1970   *Sounder,* by William H. Armstrong (Harper & Row)

1971   *Summer of the Swans,* by Betsy Byars (Viking)

1972   *Mrs. Frisby and the Rats of Nimh,* by Robert C. O'Brien (Atheneum)

1973   *Julie of the Wolves,* by Jean Craighead George (Harper & Row)

1974   *The Slave Dancer,* by Paula Fox (Bradbury)

1975   *M.C. Higgins, The Great,* by Virginia Hamilton (Macmillan)

1976   *The Grey King,* by Susan Cooper (Atheneum, McElderry)

1977   *Roll of Thunder, Hear My Cry,* by Mildred D. Taylor (Dial)

1978   *Bridge to Terabithia,* by Katherine Paterson (Crowell)

1979   *The Westing Game,* by Ellen Raskin (Dutton)

1980   *A Gathering of Days: A New England Girl's Journal, 1830-32,* by Joan Blos (Scribner's)

1981   *Jacob I Have Loved,* by Katherine Paterson (Crowell)

1982   *A Visit to William Blake's Inn: Poems for Innocent and Experienced Travelers,* by Nancy Willard (Harcourt Brace Jovanovich)

1983   *Dicey's Song,* by Cynthia Voight (Atheneum)

1984   *Dear Mr. Henshaw,* by Beverly Cleary (Morrow)

1985   *The Hero and the Crown,* by Robin McKinley (Greenwillow)

1986   *Sarah, Plain and Tall,* by Patricia MacLachlan (Harper & Row)

1987   *The Whipping Boy,* by Sid Fleischman (Greenwillow)

1988   *Lincoln: A Photobiography,* by Russell Freedman (Clarion)

1989   *Make a Joyful Noise,* by Paul Fleischman (Harper)

1990   *Number the Stars,* by Lois Lowry (Houghton Mifflin)

1991   *Maniac McGee,* by Jerry Spinelli (Little, Brown)

1992   *Shiloh,* by Phyllis Naylor (Atheneum)

Index